FABULOUS FOOD—FABULOUSLY EASY!

Do you come home from work too late and too tired to prepare a nutritious home-cooked meal? Would you love to give your hungry latchkey kids something better than peanut butter and jam? Looking for no-fuss party tips and entertaining ideas? Here's the cookbook that lets the whole family sit down to a delicious, nutritious meal that *cooks itself* while you're away! Nothing beats crockery cooking for convenient, easy, delectable home-cooked meals! Discover a delightful, flavorful variety of new dishes that make crockery cooking a year-round feast:

• Orange-Cranberry Chicken Breasts • Antipasto Bean Salad • Curried Carrot Bisque • Zippy Vegetable Dip • Shortcut Spareribs • Stuffed Cabbage • Fresh Tomato Soup • Sweet Potato Pudding • Herb-Stuffed Turkey Breast • Caramel-Apple Euphoria • and more. For simple and delicious dining, discover the one cookbook you can't afford to be without:

MABLE HOFFMAN'S ALL-NEW
CROCKERY
FAVORITES

Bantam Cookbooks
Ask your bookseller for the books you have missed.

BETTER HOMES AND GARDENS NEW COOKBOOK
(10th edition)
THE BRILLIANT BEAN by Sally Stone and Martin Stone
THE CALIFORNIA COOK: CASUALLY ELEGANT
RECIPES WITH EXHILARATING TASTE by Diane Rossen
Worthington
THE COMPLEAT I HATE TO COOK BOOK by Peg Bracken
COUNTRY BAKING by Ken Haedrich
COUNTRY BREAKFASTS by Ken Haedrich
CROCKERY COOKERY by Mable Hoffman
THE FANNIE FARMER COOKBOOK (revised 13th edition)
edited by Marion Cunningham with Jeri Laber
FIELDS OF GREENS: NEW VEGETARIAN RECIPES FROM
THE CELEBRATED GREENS RESTAURANT by Annie
Somerville
THE GREENS COOKBOOK by Deborah Madison and
Edward Espe Brown
HOME FOR THE HOLIDAYS by Ken Haedrich
THE JOSLIN DIABETES GOURMET COOKBOOK:
HEART-HEALTHY EVERYDAY RECIPES FOR FAMILY
AND FRIENDS by Bonnie Saunders Polin and Frances
Towner Giedt
MEDITERRANEAN LIGHT by Martha Rose Shulman
PROVENÇAL LIGHT by Martha Rose Shulman
RECIPES FOR DIABETICS (revised and updated edition) by
Billie Little
SPLENDID SOUPS by James Peterson

MABLE HOFFMAN'S ALL-NEW

CROCKERY
FAVORITES

by Mable and Gar Hoffman

BANTAM BOOKS

NEW YORK • TORONTO • LONDON • SYDNEY • AUCKLAND

*This edition contains the complete text
of the original trade paperback edition.*
NOT ONE WORD HAS BEEN OMITTED.

CROCKERY FAVORITES

A Bantam Book / published by arrangement with Fisher Books

*PUBLISHING HISTORY
Fisher Books edition published 1991
Bantam edition / December 1993*

ISBN 0-553-56058-1

Published simultaneously in the United States and Canada

PRINTED IN THE UNITED STATES OF AMERICA

OPM   0 9 8 7 6 5

CONTENTS

CROCKERY FAVORITES

Crockery cooking is an important part of today's busy lifestyle. It's almost like having a cook at home—fixing dinner while you're involved in other activities. Working parents like to have dinner ready when they come home to hungry children; college students can concentrate on tomorrow's exam while dinner is cooking; and retirees can enjoy a golf game, volunteer work or shopping spree. The slow-cooker is also the ideal appliance to take in your motor home or to your summer cabin. It enables you to prepare whole meals with just one appliance, freeing you of the burden of carrying numerous pots and pans.

Hearty family-style fare as well as special-occasion dishes can be cooked while you are away. Remember that there are two temperature levels on most slow-cookers—LOW or 200F (95C) and HIGH or 300F (150C). We suggest that you use LOW when you leave an unattended cooker. If you are at home and everyone is anxious for dinner, turn the control to HIGH for the last hour or two of cooking.

Resist the temptation to lift the lid from the pot while cooking. The temperature is extremely LOW and heat escapes very fast when the lid is removed, thus requiring even longer cooking time.

It isn't necessary to stir food while cooking.

Throughout this book we have offered menu suggestions, keeping in mind ease and speed of preparation. Use them as a guide to enhance your menu planning.

1

Always read and follow the manufacturer's "Use and Care" booklet that came with your cooker.

For easier clean up, use vegetable cooking spray or grease the interior of your slow-cooker before adding ingredients.

CROCKERY-COOKING BASICS

High-altitude Cooking

Most foods take longer to cook at high altitudes. If you live in an area over 3500 feet, plan on longer cooking time.

Root Vegetables

Dense vegetables such as carrots, turnips, celery root, potatoes, onions and rutabagas take longer to cook than many meats. When combining ingredients in a slow-cooker, place root vegetables on the bottom of the pot; then add meats, seasonings, other vegetables and liquid. This keeps vegetables moist during cooking and cooks them more evenly.

Dried Beans

Cooking time for dried beans varies with the specific bean as well as the ingredients cooked with them. In general, small white beans, great Northern and baby limas take much less cooking time than kidney beans and garbanzos. In some cases we suggest certain beans be cooked on HIGH instead of the low setting. Presoaking before cooking in a slow-cooker is not usually necessary, but it shortens the cooking time. Check recipes for specific directions.

Amount of Liquid

If you are a novice in slow-cooking, you will notice more liquid in the pot at the end of cooking than with traditional cooking methods. With a lower cooking temperature, liquids do not boil away; vegetables and meats are not likely to dry out. As a result, most recipes call for the addition of far less liquids.

Pasta and Rice

These products are at their best when cooked according to traditional methods or microwaved, then added to slow-cooked recipes near the end of cooking time. If cooked for many hours, they become "gummy" or fall apart.

Milk, Sour Cream and Other Dairy Products

Dairy products are delicious additions to many recipes, but in most cases should be added to the slow-cooker near the end of the cooking time. Milk usually separates and looks curdled when cooked for hours. There are a few exceptions where milk products are mixed in with other ingredients and successfully slow-cooked. We have included several that we developed.

Heat Comes From Sides of Pot

Unlike pots and pans you use on your stovetop, most slow-cookers heat from the sides instead of the bottom. Heating coils are in the outside metal shell holding the liner. When you turn it on, these coils become hot and heat the crockery liner. Others use a heating base which provides heat from the bottom. For best results, the pot should be at least half full of ingredients.

Seasonings

We omitted additional salt from recipes that call for ingredients which contain salt. Please season to taste. Experiment with using larger amounts of spices because slow-cooking produces more liquid, diluting the effect of your spices.

ADVANTAGES OF SLOW-COOKING

Food Cooks While You Are Away

Put everything in the pot, cover and cook on LOW. You can leave for the day and when you return dinner will be ready. LOW heat does not dry out or burn the food.

Exact Timing Is Not Crucial

If you are delayed in traffic on the way home, another half hour or even an hour of extra cooking time doesn't make that much difference to most recipes that are cooking on LOW. The temperature is so low that exact timing is not critical.

Saves Energy

These pots use very little electricity because the wattage is very low. You benefit because this is a cost-efficient method of meal preparation.

Ease of Preparation

Prepare vegetables and other cut ingredients the day before; wrap and refrigerate separately until needed.

Relieves After-work Stress

After a long day at work, the hassle of deciding "what to have for dinner" is avoided when you have dinner in the slow-cooker. And it's great to come home to wonderful cooking aromas.

Does Not Heat the Kitchen

Although many people associate crockery cooking with hearty winter dishes, we've included many year-round suggestions to help you keep your kitchen cool all summer.

Foods Are Moist and Flavorful

Slow-cooking avoids the usual shrinkage of meats. Meat and vegetable juices blend together, creating more flavorful dishes. You'll find inexpensive cuts of meat benefit greatly from slow-cooking.

Handy for Buffets

Prepare appetizers or main dishes in the slow-cooker. Keep the pot plugged in on LOW, and the food will be just as warm for the last guest as it was for the first.

You Can Take It With You

When going to a potluck or picnic in the park, prepare a main dish or vegetable at home. To transport it, wrap the entire hot, filled slow-cooker with lid in place in 2 layers of foil, then at least 5 layers of newspaper. Secure wrappings with tape. Place wrapped cooker upright in a paper grocery bag or small box. *Keep in upright position at all times.*

TO THICKEN
SAUCES AND GRAVY

Most main-dish slow-cooker recipes result in very flavorful juices in the bottom of the pot after meats and vegetables are removed. There are several ways to thicken these juices, then use the thickened juices as sauces to enhance the food. Each recipe indicates the exact proportion for a specific sauce. Juices are usually thickened after the meat and vegetables have been removed with a slotted spoon. In some cases, the juices can be thickened while the meat and/or vegetables are in the pot. Here are some general guidelines:

Cornstarch

After food is done, turn slow-cooker on HIGH. In a cup, dissolve cornstarch in an equal amount of water. Stir into juices in the pot. Cover and cook on HIGH 20 to 30 minutes, stirring occasionally, until thickened. Use 2 tablespoons cornstarch dissolved in 2 tablespoons cold water to thicken about 2 cups liquid.

Flour

Follow the procedure above for cornstarch. But note that the amount of flour and water are different. Use 4 tablespoons flour dissolved in 4 tablespoons water to create a medium sauce with 2 cups liquid.

Quick-cooking Tapioca

This is stirred into liquid in the slow-cooker before cooking. It thickens as the meat and vegetables cook. With 2 cups liquid, add 3 or 4 tablespoons quick-cooking tapioca.

Vegetables

In certain recipes, we mashed beans to thicken mixtures. Other times, we used potato flakes or puréed potatoes with other vegetables.

TO ENHANCE THE PRESENTATION OF SLOW-COOKED FOODS

- At serving time, sprinkle top with chopped fresh herbs, chopped tomatoes, green onions, grated cheese, buttered crumbs or crushed corn chips.
- For a stew-type dish, drop mounds of dumpling batter on top of cooked mixture; cover and cook on HIGH 30 to 45 minutes. See page 203.
- Spoon cooked-meat mixture into scooped-out French rolls;
    over toasted English muffins;
    in puffed pastry shells;
    in crisp taco shells;
    over soft flour tortillas;
    in pita rounds;
    over corn-bread squares;
    over cooked fettuccine or other pasta;
    over cooked regular, brown or wild rice;
    over baked potatoes.
- Cook meat or chicken with seasonings in slow-cooker a day ahead. Refrigerate overnight. Place in casserole. Cover with your favorite pastry recipe, refrigerated biscuits or ready-to-bake pie crust; bake according to package directions.
- Add pea pods, mushrooms and other quick-cooking vegetables near the end of cooking time.

TO BROWN OR
NOT TO BROWN

When food is prepared in a slow-cooker, it does not brown as it does in a skillet or oven. It is not necessary to brown food before slow-cooking, and we have not indicated this procedure in recipes in this book. However, if you prefer the color and flavor of browned meat, poultry, onions or other vegetables, heat a small amount of oil in a skillet; add meat or vegetables and brown on medium-high heat. Turn meat or vegetables over and brown other side. Or place in broiler pan and lightly brush with oil, if desired. Broil 4 to 6 inches from source of heat until brown; turn and broil other side. Add to mixture in slow-cooker and follow our directions for the recipe.

HOW TO REDUCE FAT IN
SLOW-COOKED MEALS

- Purchase chops and roasts with thin layers of fat.
- Carefully trim all excess fat from meats before cooking.
- Add little or no oil or fat when cooking meat or sauces.
- After cooking and before serving, skim off excess fat.
- Cool any fatty cooked meat several hours or refrigerate overnight. Lift and discard solidified fat with spoon or spatula. Then reheat mixture on stovetop, in microwave or oven.
- Before adding fatty meat to slow-cooker, quickly brown it in a skillet or in the oven. Discard drippings and follow the directions for the recipe.

FOOD SAFETY

Thaw meat or poultry in the refrigerator or microwave, following manufacturer's directions. Do not thaw at room temperature.

Wash hands and utensils between each step of food preparation.

When serving, do not let cooked foods stand at room temperature more than 2 hours. Remember, keep hot foods hot and cold foods cold. Refrigerate leftovers promptly.

Documentation

Nutrient analysis was calculated using The Food Processor II Nutrition & Diet Analysis System software program, version 3.0, copyright 1988, 1990 by ESHA Research. Analysis does not include optional ingredients. The higher number is used for the range of servings.

Abbreviations

Because words like *carbohydrates* are too long to fit the recipe in chart form, we abbreviated as follows:

Cal = Calories
Prot = Protein
Carb = Carbohydrates
Chol = Cholesterol

UNDER 6 HOURS COOKING

New owners of slow-cookers find it hard to believe that there are not very many kinds of foods that can be cooked in a slow-cooker in less than 6 hours. Most of the main dishes with large pieces of meats require longer cooking time.

Ground, chopped, thinly sliced or pounded meats cook in less than 6 hours, unless they are combined with fibrous root vegetables. If you want to serve dinner within six hours, count on your slow-cooker for Apple Pork Curry, Grand-Slam Sloppy Joes or Orange-Cranberry Chicken Breasts.

Enjoy a relaxed barbecue summer or winter. Accent our tangy Smoky Barbecue Ribs by pairing them with your favorite potato salad. Add fresh herbs to your home-made biscuits or dip the tops of prepared biscuits in a butter-herb mixture before baking. Fresh fruit of your choosing is the perfect ending to this meal.

MENU

Smoky Barbeque Ribs, page 17
Potato Salad
Cole Slaw
Herb Biscuits
Angel-food Cake
Fresh Fruit

TURKEY VEGETABLE ROUND

*Cheesecloth holds mixture together while it's going in
and out of the pot as well as during the cooking
process. If you don't have cheesecloth, use a piece of
white cotton cloth.*

1 medium potato,
   quartered, peeled
1 carrot, peeled
2 small zucchini, trimmed
1 leek
1½ lbs. ground turkey
2 eggs, beaten slightly
1 teaspoon chopped
   fresh thyme

1 teaspoon chopped
   fresh sage
1 teaspoon Dijon-style
   mustard
½ teaspoon salt
⅛ teaspoon pepper
1 tablespoon
   Worcestershire sauce

In food processor, shred potato, carrot and zucchini.
Slice leek in half lengthwise, thoroughly rinse and cut
into thin slices. Combine shredded potato, carrot and
zucchini with sliced leek, ground turkey, eggs and
remaining ingredients. Shape into a 6-inch ball. Place
rack in slow-cooker. Place meat on 9" × 24" double
thickness of cheesecloth. Gently lift into pot on rack.
Loosely fold cheesecloth over top of meat. Cover;
cook on LOW 5½ to 6 hours. Holding ends of
cheesecloth, lift cooked meat from pot. Remove
cheesecloth; cut meat into 5 or 6 wedges. Spoon
drippings over wedges. Makes 5 or 6 servings.

1 serving contains:

Cal	Prot	Carb	Fat	Chol	Sodium
279	26g	9g	15g	136mg	320mg

APPLE PORK CURRY

Real curry enthusiasts may want to add more curry powder just before thickening the mixture.

2 lbs. lean pork, cut into ½-inch cubes

1 apple, chopped, peeled, cored

1 small onion, chopped

1 garlic clove, crushed

1 teaspoon instant chicken-bouillon granules or 1 bouillon cube

1 tablespoon curry powder

⅛ teaspoon ground cinnamon

½ teaspoon ground ginger

½ teaspoon salt

½ cup orange juice

2 tablespoons cornstarch

2 tablespoons cold water

Cooked rice

Peanuts, chopped

Raisins

Coconut

Chutney

In slow-cooker, combine pork, apple, onion, garlic, bouillon, curry powder, cinnamon, ginger, salt and orange juice. Cover and cook on LOW 5 or 6 hours or until meat is tender. Turn pot on HIGH. In measuring—

cup, dissolve cornstarch in water. Stir into pork
mixture. Cover and continue cooking on HIGH stirring
occasionally, 30 to 40 minutes or until thickened.
Serve over cooked rice; sprinkle with peanuts, raisins,
coconut and chutney, if desired. Makes 5 to 6
servings.

1 serving contains:

Cal	Prot	Carb	Fat	Chol	Sodium
278	32g	8g	12g	111mg	297mg

*Frozen yogurt and slices of fresh pineapple or melon
make an ideal dessert after your curry dinner.*

SOUTH SEAS POULTRY MEATBALLS

A sweet-sour sauce with oriental overtones.

¹/₄ cup low-salt soy sauce	turkey, skinned, boned, cubed
²/₃ cup orange juice	¹/₂ cup rolled oats
¹/₂ teaspoon grated orange peel	1 (8-oz.) can sliced water chestnuts, drained
2 tablespoons hoisin sauce	1 egg
¹/₄ cup dry white wine	¹/₄ teaspoon salt
2 tablespoons honey	
1 tablespoon sesame oil	2 tablespoons cornstarch
1 garlic clove, crushed	2 tablespoons water
1¹/₂ lbs. chicken or	

In large bowl, combine soy sauce, orange juice and peel, hoisin sauce, wine, honey, oil and garlic; set aside. In food processor fitted with metal blade, process chicken or turkey until finely chopped. Add oats, water chestnuts, egg and salt. Process until water chestnuts are chopped. Form into 1¹/₄- or 1¹/₂-inch balls. Place in slow cooker. Add sauce mixture. Cover and cook on LOW 5¹/₂ to 6 hours. With slotted spoon, remove meat balls; cover and keep warm. Turn pot on HIGH. Dissolve cornstarch in water. Add to sauce in pot; cook on HIGH, stirring occasionally, 20 to 30 minutes or until thickened. Serve over meatballs. Makes about 30 meatballs.

1 meatball contains:

Cal	Prot	Carb	Fat	Chol	Sodium
55	5g	5g	2g	20mg	128mg

SMOKY BARBECUE RIBS

Use chili sauce that is similar to ketchup, not the hot spicy variety with chile peppers.

2 tablespoons balsamic
   vinegar
1 tablespoon Dijon-style
   mustard
1 tablespoon
   Worcestershire sauce
2 tablespoons brown
   sugar
1 tablespoon soy sauce
1/4 teaspoon dried red-
   pepper flakes,
   crumbled

1 teaspoon grated fresh
   ginger root
1/2 teaspoon liquid
   smoke
1 cup chili sauce
1/4 cup chopped green
   onions

4 lbs. spareribs, cut into
   individual ribs

In medium bowl, combine all ingredients except ribs.
Dip each rib into sauce or brush sauce on both sides
of ribs. Place coated ribs in slow-cooker. Pour
remaining sauce over ribs in pot. Cover and cook on
LOW 5 to 6 hours or until meat is tender. Makes 6
servings.

1 serving contains:

Cal	Prot	Carb	Fat	Chol	Sodium
542	36g	17g	36g	143mg	948mg

*Balsamic vinegar has a distinctive pungent flavor; if
not available use apple-cider vinegar.*

GRAND-SLAM SLOPPY JOES

A turkey variation of the traditional Sloppy Joe; great served on warm French rolls or hamburger buns.

1 red onion, chopped
1 yellow or green bell
   pepper, chopped
1½ lbs. boneless turkey,
   finely chopped
1 cup bottled chili sauce
   or ketchup

1 garlic clove, crushed
1 teaspoon Dijon-style
   mustard
¼ teaspoon salt
⅛ teaspoon pepper

6 French rolls

Place onion, bell pepper and turkey in slow-cooker. In small bowl, combine chili sauce or ketchup, garlic, mustard, salt and pepper. Pour over turkey-vegetable mixture; stir with fork to break up clusters of turkey. Cover and cook on LOW 4½ to 6 hours or until turkey is very tender. Use a fork to break up any large chunks of turkey. Cut French rolls in half and toast. For each serving, spoon turkey mixture over 2 halves of open-face, toasted rolls. Makes 6 servings.

1 serving contains:

Cal	Prot	Carb	Fat	Chol	Sodium
403	36g	48g	6g	66mg	1175mg

MANDARIN-STYLE PASTA

Sauce may be cooked in slow-cooker ahead of time, then reheated and added to cooked pasta at serving time.

$^1/_2$ cup hoisin sauce
3 tablespoons low-salt soy sauce
$^3/_4$ cup ketchup
$^1/_4$ cup dry sherry
1 garlic clove, crushed
2 teaspoons sesame oil
$^1/_3$ cup sliced green onion
$^1/_8$ teaspoon pepper

$1^1/_2$ lbs. uncooked turkey breast slices, cut into $^1/_4'' \times ^1/_2'' \times 1''$ strips

12 oz. angel hair (capellini) or fettuccine pasta, cooked
Toasted sesame seeds

In large bowl, combine hoisin sauce, soy sauce, ketchup, sherry, garlic, sesame oil, green onion and pepper. Stir in turkey strips. Pour into slow-cooker. Cover; cook on LOW 4$^1/_2$ to 5 hours or until turkey is tender. Spoon over cooked pasta; toss. Sprinkle with sesame seeds. Makes 6 servings.

1 serving contains:

Cal	Prot	Carb	Fat	Chol	Sodium
464	38g	60g	6g	66mg	1061mg

Hoison sauce is a dark, spicy, sweetened soybean, chile pepper and garlic mixture.

SAUSAGE-STUFFED CHICKEN WITH PINE NUTS

Flavor combinations of foods are complementary to each other.

6 chicken breast halves,
   boned, skinned
1/2 lb. Italian sausage
1 small onion, chopped
1/2 cup soft breadcrumbs
1/2 teaspoon grated
   lemon peel
1/4 cup pine nuts,
   chopped

1 tablespoon minced
   fresh parsley
1/2 teaspoon dried
   tarragon
1/4 teaspoon salt
1/8 teaspoon pepper
2 tablespoons dry white
   wine

Chopped parsley

Place one chicken breast at a time in small plastic bag or between sheets of waxed paper. Lightly pound with meat mallet; set aside. Remove casings from sausage. In medium bowl, crumble sausage; combine with onion, breadcrumbs, lemon peel, pine nuts, 1 tablespoon parsley, tarragon, salt and pepper. Divide stuffing into 6ths; form each into cylinder about 3 1/2″ × 1 1/2″. Place one on center of each pounded chicken breast. Fold over and secure with small skewer. Place rack in bottom of slow-cooker. Dip 24″ × 14″ cheesecloth into wine until moistened. Place on rack with ends extending up side of pot. Place stuffed chicken breasts on cheesecloth. Then fold ends

of cheesecloth over chicken. Cover and cook on LOW
4 hours or until chicken is tender. Holding the ends of
cheesecloth, remove chicken from pot. Remove
cheesecloth; sprinkle chicken with chopped parsley.
Makes 6 servings.

1 serving contains:

Cal	Prot	Carb	Fat	Chol	Sodium
301	34g	5g	16g	95mg	436mg

ORANGE-CRANBERRY
CHICKEN BREASTS

*Popular orange-cranberry flavor combination
enhances this presentation of chicken breasts.*

1 cup chopped fresh
   cranberries
2 tablespoons brown
   sugar
5 slices cinnamon-raisin
   bread
2 tablespoons melted
   margarine or butter

¼ teaspoon grated
   orange peel
8 chicken breast halves,
   boned, skinned
¼ cup orange juice
2 tablespoons melted
   margarine or butter

1 orange, sliced

In medium bowl, combine cranberries and brown
sugar; set aside. Toast bread; cut into ¹/₂-inch cubes.
Combine bread cubes, 2 tablespoons melted margarine
or butter, orange peel and cranberry mixture. Place
one chicken breast at a time in a small plastic bag or
between sheets of waxed paper. Lightly pound with
meat mallet. Repeat with all chicken breasts. Spoon
about ¹/₃ cup cranberry mixture on center of each.
Roll up; skewer to close. In shallow dish, combine
orange juice and 2 tablespoons melted margarine or
butter. Roll filled chicken breasts in orange-juice
mixture. Place in slow-cooker. Cover and cook on
LOW about 5 hours. To serve, spoon drippings over
chicken. Garnish with orange slices. Makes 8 servings.

1 serving contains:

Cal	Prot	Carb	Fat	Chol	Sodium
252	28g	16g	8g	73mg	194mg

When fresh cranberries are in season, buy several
packages and freeze them for later use.

STUFFED CABBAGE

Select a large head of cabbage so you'll have a number of big outside leaves. Save smaller inside leaves for cole slaw or another cabbage dish.

1 large head cabbage
1 egg, beaten slightly
1 tablespoon chopped
   fresh parsley
2 tablespoons chopped
   green onion
1 teaspoon chopped
   fresh sage
1/2 teaspoon salt
1/8 teaspoon pepper

2 slices (about 2 oz.)
   boiled or baked ham,
   chopped
2 cups (about 1 lb.)
   ground turkey
1 cup cooked rice

Bottled sweet-sour
   sauce, optional

Break off 9 or 10 large cabbage leaves. Drop into boiling water until limp. Drain and set aside. In medium bowl, combine egg, parsley, green onion, sage, salt, pepper, ham, turkey and rice. Spoon about 1/3 cup turkey mixture on each cabbage leaf. Fold in sides and roll ends over filling. Place seam-side down on rack in slow-cooker. Cover; cook on LOW 5 to 6 hours. Serve plain or with bottled sweet-sour sauce, if desired. Makes 9 or 10 rolls.

1 serving contains:

Cal	Prot	Carb	Fat	Chol	Sodium
133	12g	7g	6g	50mg	229mg

For easier rolling, trim thick base of each cabbage leaf before spooning on turkey mixture.

FRESH ARTICHOKES

Dip tender ends of leaves and artichoke bottom into sauce or squeeze lemon juice over cooked artichoke.

2 large fresh artichokes
6 cups hot water
4 thin slices lemon

Lemon-Butter Sauce:
1/3 cup melted
   margarine or butter
3 tablespoons lemon
   juice
1/4 teaspoon seasoned
   salt

With sharp knife, slice about 1 inch off top of each artichoke; cut off stem near base. With scissors, trim about ½ inch off top of each leaf. With sharp knife, halve each artichoke vertically; then scoop out and discard the fuzzy center or choke. Place artichoke halves in slow-cooker; add hot water and lemon slices. Cover and cook on HIGH 4 to 5 hours or until done. Drain; serve with sauce. Makes 4 servings.

Lemon-Butter Sauce: Combine melted margarine or butter, lemon juice and seasoned salt.

1 serving with sauce contains:

Cal	Prot	Carb	Fat	Chol	Sodium
156	4g	12g	12g	0	380mg

The artichoke is an edible bud of the cynara scolymus *thistle.*

YANKEE YAMS

Yams are compatible with the contrast of slightly tart apples accented by maple syrup.

2 tablespoons softened
   margarine or butter
5 medium yams or
   sweet potatoes
3 cooking apples,
   peeled, cored, cut
   into 8 wedges
1/4 teaspoon ground
   nutmeg

1/4 cup maple-flavored
   syrup
2 tablespoons melted
   margarine or butter

2 tablespoons chopped
   pecans, optional

Brush 2 tablespoons softened margarine or butter on bottom and about 6 inches up sides of slow-cooker. Peel yams or sweet potatoes; cut into 1/2-inch crosswise slices. Place on bottom of slow-cooker. Top with apple wedges; then nutmeg, maple syrup and 2 tablespoons melted margarine or butter. Cover and cook on LOW 3 1/2 to 4 hours or until tender. Sprinkle with pecans, if desired. Makes about 6 servings.

1 serving contains:

Cal	Prot	Carb	Fat	Chol	Sodium
219	2g	41g	6g	0	105mg

SALSA-TOPPED ONIONS

An interesting recipe to perk up a menu of bland foods. Serve with broiled chicken or fish. Cilantro, a member of the parsley family, is also known as coriander *or* Chinese parsley.

3 medium onions,
  peeled, halved
  crosswise
2 tablespoons chopped
  cilantro
1 jalapeño pepper,
  seeded, chopped
2 small tomatoes,
  peeled, seeded,
  chopped
1 garlic clove, crushed
1 tablespoon red wine
  vinegar
2 tablespoons vegetable
  oil
¼ teaspoon salt

Place onion halves cut-side up in slow-cooker. In small bowl, combine cilantro, jalapeño, tomatoes, garlic, vinegar, oil and salt. Spoon over onions. If all onions do not fit in one layer, place 3 halves on bottom and top with ½ sauce. Lightly cover with heavy-duty foil. Arrange remaining halves and sauce on top. Cover and cook on LOW 5 to 6 hours or until onions are tender. Serve warm or cold. Makes 6 servings.

1 serving contains:

Cal	Prot	Carb	Fat	Chol	Sodium
58	1g	4g	5g	0	115mg

FRESH TOMATO SOUP

Italian or plum tomatoes are ideal for this dish, but regular tomatoes may be used.

8 medium tomatoes	1 tablespoon chopped parsley
1 medium onion, chopped	2 teaspoons Worcestershire sauce
2 carrots, peeled, thinly sliced	$\frac{1}{2}$ teaspoon salt
1 garlic clove, crushed	$\frac{1}{8}$ teaspoon pepper
1 tablespoon brown sugar	3 cups chicken broth or bouillon
1 tablespoon chopped fresh basil	

Drop tomatoes in a pan of boiling water for 15 to 20 seconds; immediately rinse with cold water. Remove skins. Cut in half crosswise; squeeze out and discard seeds. Combine in slow-cooker with onions, carrots, garlic, brown sugar, basil, parsley, Worcestershire sauce, salt, pepper and broth or bouillon. Cover and cook on LOW 5 to 6 hours or until vegetables are very soft. Purée in blender or food processor fitted with metal blade. Serve in individual bowls. Makes 6 servings.

1 serving contains:

Cal	Prot	Carb	Fat	Chol	Sodium
79	4g	14g	1g	1mg	279mg

POTATO ·LEEK CORN CHOWDER

Nonfat dry milk powder gives the appearance and taste of milk without the fat and calorie count of whole milk.

3 medium potatoes, peeled, diced
1 (11-oz.) can whole-kernel corn, not drained

½ cup chopped celery
1 (1.8-oz.) pkg. leek soup mix
4 cups water

1 cup nonfat dry milk
  powder
½ cup (2 oz.) shredded

Jarlsberg or Swiss
cheese, optional

In slow-cooker, combine potatoes, corn, celery, dry leek soup mix and water. Cover and cook on LOW 5 to 6 hours or until potatoes and celery are tender. Just before serving, gradually add dry milk powder to hot soup; gently wisk until well blended. Ladle into individual bowls; sprinkle with cheese, if desired. Makes 5 or 6 servings.

1 serving contains:

Cal	Prot	Carb	Fat	Chol	Sodium
176	8g	35g	2g	3mg	631mg

Jarlsberg is a mild-flavored Norwegian cheese.

CARAMEL-APPLE EUPHORIA

Vary this people-pleasing dessert by substituting ripe peaches for apples and ¹/₈ teaspoon almond extract for cardamom.

2 medium (5 to 6 oz. each) cooking apples
¹/₂ cup apple juice
24 (about 7 oz.) caramel candy squares, unwrapped
1 teaspoon vanilla extract
¹/₈ teaspoon ground cardamom
¹/₂ teaspoon ground cinnamon
¹/₃ cup cream-style peanut butter

7 slices angel-food cake
or
1 quart vanilla ice cream

Peel, core and cut each apple into 18 wedges; set
aside. In 3½ quart or smaller slow-cooker, combine
apple juice, unwrapped caramel candies, vanilla,
cardamom and cinnamon. Drop peanut butter, 1
teaspoon at a time, over ingredients in slow-cooker;
stir. Add apple wedges; cover and cook on LOW 5
hours. Stir contents of slow-cooker thoroughly; cover
and cook on LOW 1 additional hour. Serve
approximately ⅓ cup of warm caramel-apple mixture
over a slice of angel-food cake or vanilla ice cream.
Makes 7 servings.

1 serving sauce contains:

Cal	Prot	Carb	Fat	Chol	Sodium
216	4g	32g	9g	1mg	67mg

1 serving with cake contains:

Cal	Prot	Carb	Fat	Chol	Sodium
341	7g	61g	9g	1mg	336mg

1 serving with ice cream contains:

Cal	Prot	Carb	Fat	Chol	Sodium
369	7g	50g	17g	35mg	133mg

SWEET POTATO PUDDING

Interesting dessert to serve after a dinner featuring a Hawaiian theme.

3 large sweet potatoes,
   cooked, peeled,
   cubed
¹/₂ cup brown sugar
³/₄ cup milk
2 eggs
¹/₂ teaspoon ground
   allspice
¹/₂ teaspoon ground
   cinnamon

¹/₂ teaspoon grated
   orange peel
1 tablespoon softened
   margarine or butter

Whipped cream
Chopped macadamia
   nuts or pecans

In food processor fitted with metal blade, combine cooked sweet potatoes, brown sugar, milk, eggs, allspice, cinnamon and orange peel. Process until smooth. Grease bottom and sides of slow-cooker with margarine or butter. Spoon in potato mixture. Cover and cook on HIGH 2 to 3 hours or until mixture is puffed, firm and edges begin to brown. Serve warm or

cold. Top each serving with a dab of whipped cream
and chopped nuts. Makes 5 or 6 servings.

1 serving contains:

Cal	Prot	Carb	Fat	Chol	Sodium
181	4g	34g	4g	74mg	73mg

6 TO 8 HOURS COOKING

Within this time frame, it's possible to make our Pizza Soup with all the popular pizza flavors including sausage, tomatoes, peppers, mushrooms and topped with shredded mozzarella. Or, make a Hot 'n Sour Soup with Oriental overtones.

As far as meat dishes are concerned, Traditional Spaghetti 'n Meatballs and Beef 'n Turkey Sausage Chili will cook under 8 hours. There's time to cook Fruited Flank Steak in a spicy beer sauce.

Experience the flavors and colors of Mexico in this delightful menu. Add frozen peas to your cooked rice and cover for a minute or two to heat them. If jícama is not available, substitute fresh turnip or celery sticks. Refreshing sherbet contrasts the lively dinner.

MENU

Turkey Ranchero, page 43
Steamed Rice with Peas
Mixed Green Salad
Jícama and Bell Pepper Strips
Fresh Orange Slices
Tortillas
Pineapple Sherbet

PORK ROAST WITH FENNEL AND SAGE

When buying the roast, be sure that it is not longer than the inside diameter of your slow-cooker.

1 (3-lb.) pork loin roast
¼ teaspoon salt
⅛ teaspoon pepper
4 tablespoons chopped
   fresh sage
2 fennel bulbs, sliced
   crosswise

2 tablespoons
   cornstarch
½ cup dry white wine

Have butcher cut roast through most of bone to form individual chops. Trim off most of fat. If necessary, tie roast to hold it together. Sprinkle top and sides with salt, pepper and fresh sage. Place on rack in slow-cooker; top with fennel. Cover and cook on LOW 7 to 8 hours. Remove roast and most of fennel; keep warm. Turn slow-cooker on HIGH. Dissolve cornstarch in wine. Stir into drippings. Cover and cook on HIGH 25 to 30 minutes or until thickened; stir once or twice. To serve, cut into chops. Spoon fennel over pork; then sauce over all. Makes 5 or 6 servings.

1 serving contains:

Cal	Prot	Carb	Fat	Chol	Sodium
444	50g	5g	22g	159mg	268mg

Fennel is also known as sweet anise; *it has a very mild licorice flavor.*

TRADITIONAL SPAGHETTI 'N MEATBALLS

A good choice for an old-fashioned spaghetti dinner.

1 onion, chopped
1 carrot, peeled, chopped
1 stalk celery, chopped
1 garlic clove, crushed
1 (8-oz.) can tomato sauce
1/4 cup dry red wine
2 teaspoons chopped fresh basil

2 teaspoons chopped fresh oregano
1 teaspoon chopped fresh thyme
1 teaspoon Worcestershire sauce
1/2 teaspoon salt
1/8 teaspoon pepper
1 (28-oz.) can Italian tomatoes with juice

1 lb. lean ground beef
¹/₂ lb. mild Italian
   sausage
¹/₂ cup seasoned dry
   breadcrumbs
1 egg, beaten slightly

¹/₄ cup milk

1 lb. spaghetti, cooked
Grated Parmesan
   cheese, optional

In slow-cooker, combine onion, carrot, celery, garlic,
tomato sauce, wine, basil, oregano, thyme,
Worcestershire sauce, salt and pepper. Chop tomatoes
and add to mixture in slow-cooker. In medium bowl,
combine beef, sausage, breadcrumbs, egg and milk.
Form into 20 to 22 (1¹/₂-inch) meatballs. Carefully
place in sauce in slow-cooker. Cover and cook on
LOW 7 to 8 hours. Spoon hot mixture over cooked
spaghetti or other pasta. Sprinkle with grated
Parmesan cheese, if desired. Makes 6 to 7 servings.

1 serving contains:

Cal	Prot	Carb	Fat	Chol	Sodium
483	26g	57g	16g	85mg	847mg

TURKEY RANCHERO

For variety, omit corn chips and serve turkey over cooked rice or noodles. Delicious also as a filling for tacos or tostadas. Use either corn or flour tortillas.

4 turkey thighs (4¹/₂ to
    5 lbs.)
1 (1⁵/₈-oz.) pkg.
    enchilada sauce mix
1 (6-oz.) can tomato
    paste
¹/₄ cup water

¹/₃ cup lowfat yogurt or
    dairy sour cream
¹/₄ cup sliced green
    onions
¹/₂ cup sliced ripe olives
1¹/₂ cup corn chips,
    crushed

1 cup (4 oz.) grated
    Monterey Jack cheese

With sharp knife, cut each thigh in half; remove bone and skin. Place in slow-cooker. Combine dry enchilada sauce mix with tomato paste and water. Mixture will be thick. Spread over turkey thighs. Cover; cook on LOW 7 to 8 hours or until tender. Turn pot on HIGH. Add cheese; stir until cheese melts. Spoon into an au gratin dish or shallow casserole. Spoon yogurt or sour cream over turkey. Sprinkle with green onions and olives. Top with corn chips. Makes 8 servings.

1 serving contains:

Cal	Prot	Carb	Fat	Chol	Sodium
383	42g	11g	18g	121mg	346mg

FRUITED FLANK STEAK ON RICE

Flank steak fits flat on bottom of larger slow-cooker; edges of meat will extend an inch or two up the sides of 3¹/₂-quart pot.

1 (1¹/₂ lbs.) flank steak
2 cups mixed dried fruits
2 tablespoons orange marmalade
2 tablespoons brown sugar
2 tablespoons lemon juice

¹/₄ teaspoon ground ginger
¹/₄ teaspoon ground cinnamon
1 teaspoon Worcestershire sauce
¹/₄ teaspoon salt
¹/₈ teaspoon pepper
1 (12-oz.) can beer

2 tablespoons   Cooked rice
  cornstarch
2 tablespoons cold
  water

Place whole flank steak in slow-cooker. In medium
bowl, combine dried fruits, marmalade, brown sugar,
lemon juice, ginger, cinnamon, Worcestershire sauce,
salt, pepper and beer. Pour over meat. Cover and
cook on LOW about 7 hours. With slotted spoon,
remove meat and fruit; keep warm. Turn pot on
HIGH. In small bowl, dissolve cornstarch in cold
water. Stir into juices in pot. Cover and cook on HIGH
15 to 20 minutes or until thickened, stirring
occasionally. Spoon over warm meat and fruit. Serve
on a bed of rice. Makes 6 to 7 servings.

1 serving contains:

Cal	Prot	Carb	Fat	Chol	Sodium
266	21g	27g	7g	49mg	164mg

Apple juice can be substituted for the beer.

MEAT AND POTATO LOAF

If Italian sausage is in a casing, remove the casing before adding to other ingredients.

1½ lbs. lean ground
   beef
½ lb. Italian sausage
1 small onion, chopped
1 cup instant potato
   flakes, not
   reconstituted (dry)

1 egg, beaten slightly
1 cup beef broth or
   bouillon
½ cup milk
½ teaspoon salt
½ teaspoon dried Italian
   seasoning

In large bowl, combine all ingredients. Shape into a 7-inch ball. Place a trivet in slow-cooker. Place meat ball on double thickness of cheesecloth (about 24-inches square). Holding the ends of cheesecloth, gently lower meat into pot. Loosely fold cheesecloth over top of meat. Cover; cook on LOW 6 to 7 hours. Holding ends of cheesecloth, lift meat from pot. Cut into wedges. Makes 6 or 7 wedges.

1 wedge contains:

Cal	Prot	Carb	Fat	Chol	Sodium
287	22g	7g	19g	103mg	444mg

SPOON PIZZA

Consider using other combinations of toppings such as fresh pork sausage, anchovies, Canadian bacon, olives, green peppers, etc.

2 (8-oz.) cans tomato
   sauce
2 garlic cloves
2 teaspoons dried
   oregano leaves
2 teaspoons dried basil
   leaves
1/2 teaspoon celery salt
1/4 teaspoon salt
1/8 teaspoon pepper
5 (6-inch) corn tortillas
5 teaspoons grated
   Parmesan cheese

1 medium onion, thinly
   sliced, separated into
   rings
2 large plum tomatoes,
   thinly sliced
1 1/2 oz. thinly sliced
   pepperoni
2 tablespoons chopped
   parsley
8 oz. mozzarella cheese,
   sliced

In blender or food processor fitted with metal blade,
combine tomato sauce, garlic, oregano, basil, celery

salt, salt and pepper. Process 3 minutes or until
puréed; set aside. Spread each tortilla with about 2¹/₂
tablespoons tomato purée; sprinkle each with 1
teaspoon grated Parmesan cheese. On each tortilla
spread about ¹/₅ of the following: onion rings, tomato
slices, pepperoni, parsley and mozzarella cheese. Place
each prepared tortilla in slow-cooker, one on top of
the other. Pour any remaining tomato purée over
stacked tortillas in slow-cooker. Cover; cook on LOW
7 to 8 hours. Spoon pizza into a serving bowl; or with
long-bladed knife, cut pizza into 6 or 8 wedges and
remove wedges to a serving platter with a metal
spatula. Spoon any sauce remaining in the slow-cooker
over pizza in bowl or on platter. Makes 6 or 8
servings.

1 serving contains:

Cal	Prot	Carb	Fat	Chol	Sodium
181	12g	16g	8g	18mg	825mg

SMOKED SAUSAGE
WITH RED CABBAGE
AND SWEET POTATOES

*Designed to convert the most reluctant vegetable
eaters. Serve with thin slices of pumpernickel bread.*

1 small head red
    cabbage, thinly sliced
2 medium sweet
    potatoes, peeled, cut
    into ¹/₂-inch slices
1 cooking apple, peeled,
    cored, thinly sliced
1 lb. smoked sausage
    ring, cut into 1-inch
    slices

2 tablespoons brown
    sugar
¹/₈ teaspoon ground
    cinnamon
¹/₄ cup red wine vinegar

Dijon-style or sweet-hot
    mustard

In slow-cooker, make alternate layers of cabbage,
sweet potatoes, apple and sausage. In small bowl,
combine brown sugar, cinnamon and vinegar. Pour

over ingredients in pot. Cover and cook on LOW 7 to
8 hours. Serve with mustard. Makes 5 or 6 servings.

1 serving contains:

Cal	Prot	Carb	Fat	Chol	Sodium
340	12g	22g	23g	53mg	727mg

*A German-inspired dish that combines wonderful
flavors, both spicy and sweet.*

LAMB 'N LENTIL STEW

*A stick-to-the-ribs dish for hearty appetites. Hot
biscuits and a salad complete your meal.*

1 lb. lean lamb
   shoulder, cut into
   1-inch cubes
1 garlic clove, crushed

1 lb. zucchini, cut
   crosswise into ½-inch
   slices

1 medium tomato,
  peeled, seeded, diced
1 teaspoon chopped
  fresh rosemary leaves
2 teaspoons balsamic
  vinegar
1/2 teaspoon salt

1/8 teaspoon pepper
1 cup dried lentils
3 cups beef broth or
  bouillon
2 cups water

Chopped fresh cilantro

In slow-cooker, combine all ingredients except
cilantro. Cover and cook on LOW 7 to 8 hours or
until lentils are tender. Sprinkle with cilantro. Makes
about 8 servings.

1 serving contains:

Cal	Prot	Carb	Fat	Chol	Sodium
203	22g	15g	7g	52mg	170mg

*Make a complete one-dish meal by adding Baked
Cheddar Topping, page 166.*

BEEF 'N TURKEY SAUSAGE CHILI

Sounds like an unusual combination of meats, but we hope you'll like it more than traditional chili.

1½ lbs. boneless beef chuck, diced
½ lb. turkey sausage
1 red or yellow bell pepper, seeded, chopped
1 onion, chopped
1 garlic clove, crushed
1 (6-oz.) can tomato paste
1 (12-oz.) can beer
1 teaspoon instant beef-bouillon granules
1 jalapeño pepper, seeded, minced

2 teaspoons chili powder
1 teaspoon ground cumin
¼ teaspoon salt

½ cup plain lowfat yogurt or dairy sour cream
2 tablespoons chopped fresh cilantro
¼ cup chopped green onions

In slow-cooker, combine all ingredients except garnishes. Cover and cook on LOW 7 to 8 hours or until beef is tender. Spoon into individual bowls.

Top with yogurt or sour cream, cilantro and green onions. Makes 5 or 6 servings.

1 serving contains:

Cal	Prot	Carb	Fat	Chol	Sodium
377	35g	12g	19g	117mg	676mg

LAMB CURRY

Accompany curry with chutney, chopped peanuts, raisins, shredded coconut, mandarin orange segments and chopped green onions.

1 onion, chopped
2 stalks celery, finely
   chopped
1 garlic clove, crushed
1¼ to 1½ lbs. boneless
   lamb stew meat, cut
   into 1-inch cubes
1 tablespoon curry
   powder
¼ teaspoon ground
   mace

½ teaspoon ground
   coriander
½ teaspoon salt
1 cup chicken broth or
   bouillon

1 tablespoon cornstarch
1 tablespoon cold water

Cooked rice

In slow-cooker, combine onion, celery and garlic. Add lamb, curry powder, mace, coriander, salt and broth or bouillon. Cover and cook on LOW 7 to 8 hours. Turn pot on HIGH. Dissolve cornstarch in water. Stir into cooked curry. Cover and cook on HIGH 15 or 20 minutes, stirring occasionally. Serve over cooked rice. Makes 5 to 6 servings.

1 serving contains:

Cal	Prot	Carb	Fat	Chol	Sodium
155	21g	3g	6g	64mg	239mg

SMOKY KIDNEY BEANS

Kidney beans have a very dense texture. They are at their best when cooked on HIGH.

1 lb. dried kidney
    beans, rinsed
6 cups water
1 medium onion,
    chopped
1/2 lb. smoked sausage
    (Keilbasa), diced

1/4 cup brown sugar,
    lightly packed
2 tablespoons Dijon-
    style mustard
1 teaspoon
    Worcestershire sauce
1 garlic clove, crushed

¹/₃ cup molasses   ¹/₂ teaspoon salt
¹/₃ cup ketchup   ¹/₈ teaspoon pepper
¹/₈ teaspoon ground
  cloves

In slow-cooker, combine dried beans and water; let stand overnight or at least 8 hours. Drain; reserve 2¹/₂ cups liquid from beans. In slow-cooker, combine drained beans, remaining ingredients and reserved 2¹/₂ cups of liquid. Cover and cook on HIGH about 7 hours or until beans are tender. Makes about 8 cups.

1 cup contains:

Cal	Prot	Carb	Fat	Chol	Sodium
303	14g	44g	9g	19mg	621mg

RED CABBAGE AND APPLES

If you're using a 3¹/₂-quart slow-cooker, be sure to use a small head of cabbage; a large amount of cabbage will not fit.

1 head red cabbage,
  thinly sliced
2 apples, seeded,
  chopped
1 medium onion,
  chopped
1 tablespoon brown
  sugar

¹/₄ teaspoon salt
¹/₈ teaspoon pepper
¹/₈ teaspoon ground
  mace
¹/₄ cup dry red wine
¹/₂ cup apple juice

Combine cabbage, apples, onion, brown sugar, salt, pepper and mace in slow-cooker. Pour wine and apple juice over all. Cover and cook on LOW 6¹/₂ to 7 hours. Serve as an accompaniment to pork roast or chops. Makes about 6 cups.

1 cup contains:

Cal	Prot	Carb	Fat	Chol	Sodium
68	1g	15g	0	0	98mg

Our version of a classic German side-dish traditionally served with venison.

GINGERY TOMATO SOUP

_A light soup that makes an interesting first course
for dinner._

1 (14½-oz.) can Italian-
    style tomatoes,
    coarsely chopped,
    not drained
1 (6-oz.) can tomato
    paste
1 garlic clove, crushed
1 red or yellow bell
    pepper, seeded,
    chopped
1 tablespoon chopped
    crystallized ginger
1 teaspoon grated
    orange peel

½ cup orange juice
⅛ teaspoon ground
    ginger
2 cups chicken broth or
    bouillon
1 tablespoon brown
    sugar
¼ teaspoon salt
⅛ teaspoon pepper

1 orange, cut in thin
    slices

In slow-cooker, combine all ingredients except orange
slices. Cover and cook on LOW 7 to 8 hours. Purée in
blender or food processor fitted with metal blade.

Serve in individual bowls. Garnish each with orange slice. Makes 5 servings.

1 serving contains:

Cal	Prot	Carb	Fat	Chol	Sodium
98	5g	20g	1g	0	264mg

Orange and tomato flavors enhance one another. Try this and see for yourself what a treat it is.

PIZZA SOUP

Unmistakable flavors in a different form. Serve with garlic bread and a mixed green salad.

2 (14-oz.) cans Italian-
style sliced tomatoes

2 cups beef broth or
bouillon

1 onion, sliced
1 small red or green bell
pepper, seeded,
sliced
1 cup sliced mushrooms
¹/₂ lb. smoked sausage
links, thinly sliced

1 teaspoon chopped
fresh oregano

1 cup (4 oz.) shredded
mozzarella or
Cheddar cheese

In slow-cooker, combine tomatoes, broth or bouillon, onion, pepper, mushrooms, sausage and oregano. Cover and cook on LOW 7 to 8 hours. Spoon into individual bowls. Top with cheese. Makes 6 to 7 servings.

1 serving contains:

Cal	Prot	Carb	Fat	Chol	Sodium
188	11g	7g	13g	32mg	576mg

HOT 'N SOUR SOUP

A light, pleasingly spicy soup with stick-to-the-ribs ingredients.

½ lb. lean pork, cut into thin strips

¼ lb. (about 7) fresh mushrooms, sliced

1 (8-oz.) can sliced water chestnuts, drained

½ cup bamboo shoots, cut into strips

2 tablespoons rice wine vinegar

2 tablespoons soy sauce

1 teaspoon sesame oil

¼ teaspoon dried red-pepper flakes

1 cup cubed firm tofu, cut into ½-inch cubes

2 cups chicken broth or bouillon

2 cups water

Green onion slices for garnish

In slow-cooker, combine all ingredients except green onions. Cover; cook on LOW 7 to 8 hours. Ladle into individual bowls. Garnish with green-onion slices. Makes 7 to 8 servings.

1 serving contains:

Cal	Prot	Carb	Fat	Chol	Sodium
108	11g	6g	5g	22mg	282mg

Bamboo shoots can be found canned in the Oriental-food section of your market.

COUNTRY-STYLE CHICKEN SOUP

Large proportion of chicken provides a hearty main dish.

1 (3- to 4-lb.) chicken,
  cut up
1 onion or leek,
  chopped
1 carrot, finely chopped
1/2 cup chopped celery
2 tablespoons chopped
  fresh parsley
1 bay leaf

1 teaspoon chopped
  fresh thyme
1/2 teaspoon salt
1/8 teaspoon pepper
6 cups water

4 oz. cooked fine egg
  noodles or 3 cups
  cooked rice

In 4-quart or larger slow-cooker, combine chicken,
onion or leek, carrot, celery, parsley, bay leaf, thyme,
salt, pepper and water. Cover and cook on LOW 7 or
8 hours or until tender. Remove chicken and bay leaf.
Turn cooker on HIGH. Remove meat from chicken
parts; cut into bite-size pieces. Return chicken to
slow-cooker; add cooked noodles or rice. Serve when
heated to desired temperature. Makes 8 or 9 servings.

1 serving contains:

Cal	Prot	Carb	Fat	Chol	Sodium
188	23g	10g	6g	74mg	183mg

POTATO LEEK SOUP

Slow-cooker variation of a popular soup featuring potatoes and leeks.

3 medium potatoes, peeled, chopped
1 carrot, peeled, finely chopped
2 leeks, washed, sliced crosswise
1 teaspoon chopped fresh thyme

¹/₄ teaspoon salt
¹/₈ teaspoon pepper
4 cups chicken broth or bouillon

1 cup dairy sour cream
Ground nutmeg

In slow-cooker, combine potatoes, carrot, leeks, thyme, salt, pepper and broth or bouillon. Cover and cook on LOW 6 or 7 hours or until potatoes are soft. Stir in sour cream. Spoon into soup bowls; sprinkle with nutmeg. Makes about 8 servings.

1 serving contains:

Cal	Prot	Carb	Fat	Chol	Sodium
147	5g	17g	7g	13mg	93mg

Although leeks look strong, their flavor is very mild.

GREEN CHILE CORN CHOWDER

Hearty, attractive green-and-gold soup with flecks of red.

1 (15- or 16½-oz.) can cream-style corn

2 potatoes, peeled, diced

2 tablespoons chopped fresh chives

1 (4-oz.) can diced green chiles, drained

1 (2oz.) jar pimientos, chopped

½ cup chopped ham

3 cups chicken broth or bouillon

1 cup milk or light cream

1 cup (4 oz.) shredded Monterey Jack cheese

In slow-cooker, combine corn, potatoes, chives, chiles, pimientos, ham and broth or bouillon. Cover and cook on LOW 7 to 8 hours or until potatoes are tender. Stir in milk or light cream. Reheat, if desired. Serve in individual bowls; sprinkle with shredded cheese. Makes 8 servings.

1 serving contains:

Cal	Prot	Carb	Fat	Chol	Sodium
170	10g	20g	6g	20mg	507mg

PORK 'N CELLOPHANE
NOODLE SOUP

Good choice for an unusual soup. The noodles add extra interest.

½ lb. lean pork, cut into ½-inch cubes

2 medium turnips, peeled, cut into ¼″ × 2″ strips

1 medium carrot,

peeled, thinly sliced crosswise

3 green onions, cut into ½-inch pieces

2 teaspoons soy sauce

2 tablespoons sherry

¹/₈ teaspoon pepper
4 cups chicken broth or
 bouillon

2 oz. cellophane
 noodles, broken into
 3- or 4-inch lengths

In slow-cooker, combine all ingredients except
noodles. Cover and cook on LOW 6 to 7 hours. About
15 minutes before serving, place noodles in a large
saucepan or heat-proof bowl; cover with boiling
water. Let stand 10 minutes. Drain; add to mixture in
slow-cooker. Ladle into individual bowls. Makes 6 to 7
servings.

1 serving contains:

Cal	Prot	Carb	Fat	Chol	Sodium
99	10g	5g	4g	25mg	140mg

*Cellophane or transparent noodles are widely used
in both Chinese and Japanese cuisines. In India they
are called* China Grass.

GARDEN GATE SOUP

Apples team up with vegetables for this smooth, mouth-watering soup.

1 to 1¹/₂ lbs. banana
    squash, peeled,
    seeded, cubed
1 cooking apple, peeled,
    cubed
1 large sweet potato,
    peeled, cubed
1 small onion, sliced
1 teaspoon curry
    powder

2 teaspoons
    Worcestershire sauce
3 cups apple juice
¹/₄ teaspoon salt

¹/₃ cup dairy sour cream
    or plain yogurt,
    stirred
Ground nutmeg

In slow-cooker, combine squash, apple, potato, onion, curry powder, Worcestershire sauce, apple juice and salt. Cover and cook on LOW 6 to 7 hours or until vegetables are tender. Purée, half at a time, in blender or food processor fitted with metal blade. Stir in sour cream or yogurt. Sprinkle with nutmeg. Makes about 6 servings.

1 serving contains:

Cal	Prot	Carb	Fat	Chol	Sodium
160	3g	32g	3g	6mg	123mg

PIÑA COLADA BREAD PUDDING

If you prefer to serve this dessert cold, spoon into serving dish, cover and refrigerate; then eat later.

1 (1-lb.) unsliced loaf French or sourdough bread

1 (10-oz.) can frozen Piña Colada drink mix

1 (6-oz.) can pineapple juice

1 (12-oz.) can evaporated skimmed milk

½ cup cream of coconut

2 (7 or 8 oz. each) ripe bananas, sliced crosswise

3 eggs

⅓ cup Irish cream or ¼ cup light rum, optional

1 cup golden raisins

1 (8-oz.) can crushed pineapple and juice

1 teaspoon grated lemon peel

8 or 10 fresh mint sprigs

With sharp knife, peel crust from bread; discard crust or make into breadcrumbs for use in another recipe. Cut bread into 1-inch cubes; set aside. In blender or food processor fitted with metal blade, combine *half* of following ingredients: drink mix, pineapple juice, milk, cream of coconut and banana slices. Process until puréed; pour purée into 6-cup bowl. Purée remaining half of liquid ingredients and banana slices as well as eggs and liqueur, if desired. Combine both purées. Combine raisins and crushed pineapple with juice; set aside. Place about ²/₃ of bread cubes in slow-cooker; sprinkle ¹/₂ teaspoon grated lemon peel and spread 1 cup raisin-pineapple mixture over bread in slow-cooker. Top with remaining bread cubes; then with remaining lemon peel and raisin-pineapple mixture. Pour puréed ingredients into slow-cooker. Cover and cook on LOW 6 hours. Spoon pudding into 8 or 10 dessert dishes and serve hot. Garnish with mint. Makes 8 or 10 servings.

1 serving contains:

Cal	Prot	Carb	Fat	Chol	Sodium
362	10g	60g	8g	65mg	345mg

8 TO 10 HOURS COOKING

Tantalizing aromas will permeate your home all day if you choose a recipe in this chapter. These dishes lend themselves to long slow-cooking to bring out the maximum flavor of those tender morsels.

There's a potpourri of flavors, including several soups and stews. Also included are hearty dishes that are too thick to be called a *soup,* usually under the label of chili or stews.

A delicious wholesome stew you can serve direct from the pot. Fresh vegetables lend extra texture and color. Dip crusty French bread into the hearty sauce. For a refreshing finale serve your favorite ice cream and offer a variety of toppings.

MENU

Lamb Ragout, page 79
Sliced Tomatoes
Celery and Zucchini Sticks
French Bread
Ice Cream Sundaes
Cookies

ANGEL HAIR PASTA SOUP

For a variety in pasta, try cheese-filled ravioli or other fresh refrigerated pastas found in the deli or dairy section of your market.

1 onion, quartered
1 medium celery root, peeled, cubed
1 garlic clove
1 teaspoon chopped fresh thyme
1 carrot, peeled, quartered
1 tablespoon coarsely chopped fresh parsley
1 (28-oz.) can Italian-style tomatoes

2 oz. prosciutto ham, coarsely chopped
5 cups chicken broth or bouillon

4 oz. angel hair (capellini) pasta, broken into 3- or 4-inch lengths
Grated Parmesan cheese

In food processor fitted with metal blade, combine onion, celery root, garlic, thyme, carrot and parsley. Process until finely chopped but not puréed; remove. Repeat process with tomatoes and prosciutto. Combine chopped ingredients and broth or bouillon in slow-cooker. Cover; cook on LOW 8 to 9 hours. Turn on HIGH. Add pasta; cover and cook on HIGH 20 to 25 minutes or until pasta is tender. Ladle into individual bowls; sprinkle with Parmesan cheese. Makes 8 to 10 servings.

1 serving contains:

Cal	Prot	Carb	Fat	Chol	Sodium
98	7g	15g	2g	4mg	247mg

Capellini (capelli d'angelo), which means angel hair, is the thinnest variety of pasta.

LENTIL CHILI

For an interesting change, serve over baked potatoes.

1 lb. beef or lamb stew meat, cubed
1 (14½-oz.) can chopped, peeled tomatoes
1 (8-oz.) can tomato sauce

1 onion, chopped
1 garlic clove, crushed
½ teaspoon ground cumin
2 teaspoons chili powder

2 tablespoons chopped
fresh cilantro leaves

2 tablespoons balsamic
vinegar

1 cup dried lentils,
rinsed

$^1\!/_2$ teaspoon salt

$^1\!/_3$ cup plain lowfat
yogurt, stirred

Cilantro sprigs

In slow-cooker, combine all ingredients except yogurt
and cilantro sprigs. Cover and cook on LOW 8 to 9
hours. Garnish with yogurt and cilantro sprigs. Makes
5 to 6 servings.

1 serving contains:

Cal	Prot	Carb	Fat	Chol	Sodium
274	29g	26g	6g	55mg	568mg

*Lentils are available in colors varying from green to
yellow, orange or brown. Presoaking is not necessary
before cooking.*

POTATO SHIITAKE SOUP

You may want to serve this soup without puréeing; it's equally delicious when it has lots of texture.

1 oz. dried shiitake mushrooms, chopped

4 medium potatoes, peeled and cubed

1 small onion, diced

1 cup chopped uncooked chicken or turkey

6 cups chicken broth or bouillon

2 tablespoons chopped fresh celery leaves

1 teaspoon Worcestershire sauce

$1/2$ teaspoon salt

$1/8$ teaspoon pepper

Dairy sour cream

Fresh celery leaves for garnish

In slow-cooker, combine chopped mushrooms, potatoes, onions, chicken or turkey, broth or bouillon, 2 tablespoons celery leaves, Worcestershire sauce, salt and pepper. Cover and cook on LOW 8 to 9 hours or until potatoes are soft. Process, half at a time, in blender or food processor fitted with metal blade until finely chopped but not smooth. Garnish each serving with a dab of sour cream and celery leaves. Makes 9 cups.

1 cup contains:

Cal	Prot	Carb	Fat	Chol	Sodium
118	9g	16g	2g	14mg	160mg

GINGERED CARROT
LEEK VICHYSSOISE

As an alternative to sour cream, add half and half or whipping cream to cooked mixture.

3 medium carrots,
  peeled, shredded
2 leeks, washed, sliced
  crosswise
3 potatoes, peeled,
  cubed
2 teaspoons grated fresh
  ginger root

$^1/_4$ teaspoon salt
$^1/_8$ teaspoon pepper
4 cups chicken broth or
  bouillon

$^1/_2$ cup dairy sour cream
Shredded carrot for
  garnish, optional

In slow-cooker, layer carrots, leeks and potatoes. Sprinkle with fresh ginger root, salt and pepper. Pour chicken broth or bouillon over all. Cover and cook on LOW 9 to 10 hours. Purée, half at a time, in blender or food processor fitted with metal blade. Gradually stir puréed mixture into sour cream. Reheat in microwave or on stovetop, if desired. Sprinkle shredded carrot on top, if desired. Makes about 6 servings.

1 serving contains:

Cal	Prot	Carb	Fat	Chol	Sodium
166	6g	25g	5g	9mg	122mg

TRADITIONAL BOLOGNESE SAUCE

Spoon over any cooked pasta from spaghetti to more interesting shapes such as bow ties or spirals. Label and freeze excess sauce for another time.

1 lb. lean ground beef
½ lb. Italian sausage, casing removed
1 onion, chopped
1 clove garlic, crushed
1 small carrot, grated
2 stalks celery, chopped
1 small green or red bell pepper, seeded, chopped
1 (28-oz.) can diced, peeled tomatoes
2 (6-oz.) cans tomato paste

1 teaspoon sugar
1 tablespoon chopped fresh oregano
1 tablespoon chopped fresh basil
1 teaspoon salt
¼ teaspoon pepper
½ cup dry red wine

Cooked pasta
Parmesan cheese, optional

Turn slow-cooker on HIGH. Add ground beef and sausage. Cook and stir until meat is broken up into small pieces. Turn pot on LOW. Add remaining ingredients, except pasta and cheese. Cover and cook

on LOW 8 to 9 hours. Makes about 8 cups. Spoon
over your favorite pasta. Sprinkle with grated
Parmesan cheese, if desired.

1 cup contains:

Cal	Prot	Carb	Fat	Chol	Sodium
253	17g	16g	14g	52mg	746mg

*Bologna, Italy is thought to be the birthplace of this
versatile sauce.*

CREAMY ROQUEFORT ONION SOUP

If you enjoy more texture in your soup, process cooked vegetables until they're finely chopped but not smooth.

4 large onions, cut into 8ths

2 medium potatoes, peeled, cubed

¼ cup margarine or butter

3 cups water

2 chicken bouillon cubes or 2 teaspoons

instant chicken granules

¼ teaspoon pepper

2 cups milk or light cream

½ cup (2 oz.) Roquefort cheese, crumbled

In slow-cooker, combine onions, potatoes, margarine or butter, water, bouillon and pepper. Cover and cook on LOW 8 to 9 hours or until vegetables are tender. Purée, half at a time, in blender or food processor fitted with metal blade. Add milk or cream. Reheat to desired temperature in microwave or in saucepan on stove. Spoon into individual bowls. Top with Roquefort cheese. Makes about 8 cups.

1 cup contains:

Cal	Prot	Carb	Fat	Chol	Sodium
136	5g	12g	8g	12mg	510mg

LAMB RAGOUT

If cooked vegetables cool while you're thickening the sauce, reheat them in the microwave before returning to the slow-cooker.

4 medium carrots, peeled, cut into crosswise slices
3 medium turnips, peeled, cut into 8ths
1½ lbs. lamb stew meat in 1-inch cubes
8 small new red potatoes, halved, not peeled
1 tablespoon chopped fresh parsley
1 garlic clove, crushed

½ teaspoon salt
⅛ teaspoon pepper
1 teaspoon chopped fresh marjoram
1 cup beef broth or bouillon
½ cup dry white wine

2 tablespoons cornstarch
3 tablespoons cold water

Place carrots and turnips on bottom of slow-cooker. Top with lamb and potatoes. In small bowl, combine parsley, garlic, salt, pepper, marjoram, broth or bouillon and wine. Pour over ingredients in pot. Cover and cook on LOW 8 to 9 hours. Turn pot on HIGH. Remove vegetables and meat with slotted spoon; keep warm. In small bowl, dissolve cornstarch in water. Stir into liquid in pot. Cover and cook on HIGH 15 to 20 minutes, stirring occasionally. Return vegetables and meat to pot; serve. Makes 6 to 7 servings.

1 serving contains:

Cal	Prot	Carb	Fat	Chol	Sodium
248	23g	22g	6g	65mg	253mg

Ragout *is the French term for a stew.*

FRESH VEGETABLE SOUP WITH PASTA

Thanks to a variety of fresh vegetables, this is a nutritious as well as good-tasting soup.

1 medium onion, chopped

2 carrots, peeled, thinly sliced

2 zucchini, sliced

2 medium tomatoes, peeled, seeded, chopped

2 (10½-oz.) cans condensed beef broth

2 cups water

2 tablespoons chopped fresh parsley

1 tablespoon chopped fresh oregano

½ cup small shell-shaped pasta

Grated Parmesan cheese

In slow-cooker, combine onion, carrots, zucchini, tomatoes, condensed beef broth, water, parsley and oregano. Cover and cook on LOW 8 to 9 hours or until vegetables are tender. Turn on HIGH. Add pasta; cover and cook on HIGH 20 minutes or until pasta is tender. Ladle into serving bowls; sprinkle with cheese. Makes 6 or 7 servings.

1 serving contains:

Cal	Prot	Carb	Fat	Chol	Sodium
61	3g	12g	1g	0	275mg

SOUTHWESTERN BLACK BEAN SOUP

A hearty soup enhanced by the flavor of ham.

1 lb. dried black beans, rinsed
6 cups beef broth or bouillon
1 large onion, chopped
2 jalapeño peppers, seeded, chopped
1 garlic clove, crushed
1 teaspoon ground cumin
1 teaspoon ground oregano

1 teaspoon ground thyme
1/8 teaspoon ground cloves
2 (about 1-lb. each) ham hocks

1/3 cup dairy sour cream or plain yogurt
1 large tomato, chopped

In slow-cooker, combine dried beans, broth or bouillon, onions, jalapeño peppers, garlic, cumin, oregano, thyme, cloves and ham hocks. Cover and cook on LOW 9 to 10 hours or until beans are tender. Remove ham hocks; cool. Shred lean meat; discard skin, bones and fat. Return shredded lean ham to pot and reheat on HIGH, if necessary. Spoon mixture into individual soup bowls.

Top each with sour cream and chopped tomato. Makes 6 to 8 servings.

1 serving contains:

Cal	Prot	Carb	Fat	Chol	Sodium
233	17g	29g	6g	15mg	247mg

In Puerto Rico, black bean soup is traditionally served with a dash of vinegar and a garnish of white rice and chopped egg.

ADRIATIC CABBAGE SOUP

A sprinkle of grated Romano cheese gives a classy finishing touch.

¹/₄ lb. salami, diced
1 carrot, peeled, finely
  chopped
1 garlic clove, crushed
³/₄ cup diced ham
1 tablespoon white
  wine vinegar
1 cup thinly sliced

fennel with some
  tops
4 cups water

1 small head (about 6
  cups) savoy cabbage,
  thinly sliced

In slow-cooker, combine salami, carrot, garlic, ham, vinegar, fennel and water. Cover and cook on LOW 8 to 10 hours. Turn pot on HIGH; add cabbage. Cover and cook on HIGH 30 minutes or until cabbage is tender. Makes about 6 servings.

1 serving contains:

Cal	Prot	Carb	Fat	Chol	Sodium
104	9g	7g	5g	21mg	492mg

TODAY'S BEEF STEW

Take advantage of the opportunity to use tender baby carrots, tiny white onions and unpeeled new potatoes.

10 (about ½ lb.) small new potatoes, halved but not peeled

12 small white onions, peeled

30 (about ½ lb.) baby carrots

1 red or green bell pepper, cut into 1-inch pieces

1½ lbs. beef stew meat, cut into 1- to 1½-inch cubes

2 cups beef broth or bouillon

2 teaspoons chopped fresh oregano leaves

¼ teaspoon paprika

1 tablespoon chopped fresh parsley

1 tablespoon Worcestershire sauce

½ teaspoon salt

⅛ teaspoon pepper

3 tablespoons cornstarch

3 tablespoons cold water

Place potatoes, onions and baby carrots in slow-cooker. Add bell pepper and beef. In small bowl, combine broth or bouillon, oregano, paprika, parsley, Worcestershire sauce, salt and pepper. Pour over meat and vegetables. Cover and cook on LOW 9 to 10 hours. Turn pot on HIGH. In small bowl, dissolve cornstarch in water; stir into cooked stew mixture. Cover and cook on HIGH 15 to 20 minutes or until thickened, stirring occasionally. Makes 6 or 7 servings.

1 serving contains:

Cal	Prot	Carb	Fat	Chol	Sodium
229	25g	15g	7g	70mg	303mg

LENTIL 'N HAM POT

A wholesome main dish that's ideal for a cold day.

2 (about 8 to 10 oz. each) ham hocks

3 cups chicken broth or bouillon

2 cups water

1 small celery root, cut into 2" × ½" × ¼" slices

2 medium carrots, peeled, thinly sliced

1 leek, washed, sliced crosswise

½ small head cabbage, sliced

1 (8-oz.) can tomato sauce

1 garlic clove, crushed

1 teaspoon paprika

1 teaspoon chopped fresh marjoram

⅛ teaspoon pepper

1 cup dried lentils, rinsed

½ cup plain yogurt

In slow-cooker, combine all ingredients except yogurt. Cover and cook on LOW 9 to 10 hours or until vegetables and lentils are tender. Remove ham hocks; cool. Discard skin, bones and fat; cut lean meat into small pieces. Return lean meat to pot and reheat on HIGH, if necessary. Spoon into individual bowls; top with yogurt. Makes about 8 servings.

1 serving contains:

Cal	Prot	Carb	Fat	Chol	Sodium
186	15g	24g	4g	12mg	444mg

SPICY KUMQUAT RELISH

A special recipe designed for a 1-quart Crock-Ette®. If you double or triple the recipe and cook in larger cooker, make sure the pot is half full.

2 cups (about 10 oz.) kumquats, sliced crosswise

½ cup dried apple chips

2 tablespoons thinly

sliced crystallized
ginger
³/₄ cup brown sugar
2 tablespoons honey
¹/₄ teaspoon ground
allspice
2 tablespoons cider
vinegar

¹/₄ cup golden raisins
¹/₄ teaspoon dried red-
pepper flakes
¹/₂ cup coarsely
chopped dried
apricots

In 1-quart slow-cooker, combine all ingredients. Cover
and cook on LOW 8 to 9 hours. Cool; serve as an
accompaniment to pork or chicken. Makes about 2
cups.

1 tablespoon contains:

Cal	Prot	Carb	Fat	Chol	Sodium
44	0	12g	0	0	5mg

*Wrap fresh kumquats in plastic and store in your
refrigerator for weeks.*

OVER 10 HOURS COOKING

Dried beans are associated with long cooking, and some varieties take longer than others. Larger and/or more dense shapes take the maximum time to become tender. We've made preparation easier by omitting the conventional overnight soaking. This worked well, with the exception of recipes having a high sugar content. Note that Sweet-Hot Bean Casserole, one of our favorites, requires overnight soaking *before* slow cooking. For higher altitudes, you may find presoaking reduces cooking time.

Slow-cookers are ideal for making stock, so we included the basic three.

There are times when you want to savor the taste of plain foods at their best. Here is our version of the classic New England boiled dinner. The crunchy salad contrasts the tender vegetables. Old-fashioned blueberry cobbler adds the final touch.

MENU

Tomato-juice Cocktail
New England "Boiled" Dinner, page 95
Mustard and Horseradish
Waldorf Salad
Hot Rolls
Blueberry Cobbler

TRADITIONAL BAKED BEANS

Good old-fashioned baked beans without soaking ahead of time.

1 lb. dried small white beans, rinsed
4½ cups water
⅓ cup molasses
¼ cup brown sugar
1 onion, chopped

¼ lb. salt pork, cut into 1-inch cubes
1 tablespoon Dijon-style mustard
½ teaspoon salt

In slow-cooker, combine all ingredients. Cover and cook on LOW 13 to 14 hours, stirring occasionally, if possible. Makes 6 to 8 servings.

1 serving contains:

Cal	Prot	Carb	Fat	Chol	Sodium
299	15g	44g	8g	12mg	391mg

For added nutrition serve protein-rich beans with a grain such as rice or a multigrain or corn bread.

AMALFI GARBANZO STEW

If possible, use fresh basil and thyme for flavor dividends.

1 lb. dried garbanzo
  beans, rinsed
5 cups water
1 (6-oz.) can tomato
  paste
¹/₂ cup dry white wine
1 tablespoon chopped
  fresh basil or 1
  teaspoon dried
1 garlic clove, crushed
2 carrots, peeled, sliced
  crosswise
1 teaspoon fresh thyme
  or ¹/₄ teaspoon dried

1 green or yellow bell
  pepper, seeded,
  sliced
¹/₂ teaspoon salt
¹/₈ teaspoon pepper
4 thin slices pepperoni,
  chopped
3 chicken breast halves,
  boned, skinned, cut
  into ¹/₂″ × 1″ pieces

1 cup (4 oz.) shredded
  mozzarella cheese

In slow-cooker, combine dried beans, water, tomato paste, wine, basil, garlic, carrots, thyme, bell peppers, salt, pepper, pepperoni and chicken. Cover and cook on LOW 10 to 12 hours or until beans are tender. Spoon into individual bowls. Sprinkle with cheese. Makes 6 to 8 servings.

1 serving contains:

Cal	Prot	Carb	Fat	Chol	Sodium
301	20g	38g	7g	23mg	296mg

Serve a crusty bread with this delicious Italian stew.

COUNTRY LIMA BEAN
& CABBAGE SOUP

High in fiber and low in fat, a robust dish.

1 lb. dried baby lima
  beans, rinsed
8 cups chicken broth or
  bouillon
1 onion, chopped
1 teaspoon chopped
  fresh marjoram
1 garlic clove, crushed

½ teaspoon dried red-
  pepper flakes,
  crushed
½ teaspoon salt
⅛ teaspoon pepper
3 cups shredded
  cabbage

In slow-cooker, combine all ingredients. Cover and
cook on LOW 10 to 11 hours or until beans are
tender. Ladle into individual bowls. Makes 8 to 9
servings.

1 serving contains:

Cal	Prot	Carb	Fat	Chol	Sodium
144	12g	21g	2g	1mg	125mg

SWEET-HOT BEAN CASSEROLE

If possible, stir the beans once while they are cooking. Crushed gingersnaps help create a marvelous sauce.

1 lb. dried great
   Northern beans,
   rinsed
6 cups water
1 cup crushed
   gingersnaps (about
   16)
2 tablespoons sweet-hot
   mustard

1 tablespoon
   Worcestershire sauce
1/2 cup molasses
3 green onions,
   chopped
1/2 teaspoon salt
1/8 teaspoon pepper

In slow-cooker, combine dried beans and water; let stand overnight or at least 8 hours. Drain; reserve 2 1/2 cups liquid from beans. In slow-cooker, combine drained beans, reserved liquid, crushed gingersnaps, mustard, Worcestershire sauce, molasses, green onions, salt and pepper. Cover and cook on LOW about 10 hours. Makes 6 to 7 servings.

1 serving contains:

Cal	Prot	Carb	Fat	Chol	Sodium
339	12g	58g	7g	8mg	345mg

NEW ENGLAND "BOILED" DINNER

Serve this traditional corned-beef dinner in the pot along with your favorite horseradish and mustard. You'll need a 4-quart or larger pot for this recipe or use less vegetables in a smaller pot.

6 medium carrots, peeled, cut into 1-inch lengths

6 medium potatoes, peeled, quartered

2 turnips or parsnips, peeled, cut into 8ths

2 large onions, peeled, quartered

1 (2- to 3-lbs.) corned-beef brisket

5 cups water

1 small head cabbage, cut into 6 wedges

In slow-cooker, combine carrots, potatoes, turnips or parsnips and onions. Top with corned beef, fat-side up. Pour water over all. Cover and cook on LOW 10 to 11 hours or until meat is tender. Remove cooked meat and vegetables; keep warm. Turn pot on HIGH; add cabbage. Cover and cook on HIGH 20 to 30 minutes or until cabbage is done. Lift cabbage with slotted spoon. Arrange on large platter with corned beef and other vegetables. Makes 6 servings.

1 serving contains:

Cal	Prot	Carb	Fat	Chol	Sodium
406	43g	39g	9g	92mg	140mg

PORK GARBANZO
MEAL-IN-A-POT

Just toss everything in the pot and forget about it until dinner time. These ingredients almost reach the top of a 3¹/₂-quart slow-cooker but will cook perfectly.

1 lb. dried garbanzo
    beans, rinsed
3 cups chicken broth or
    bouillon
3 cups water
4 large tomatoes,
    peeled, seeded,
    chopped

³/₄ lb. lean pork, cut
    into ¹/₂-inch cubes
3 oz. prosciutto,
    chopped
1 onion, chopped
1 garlic clove, crushed

1 yellow or green bell
  pepper, seeded,
  chopped
2 teaspoons chopped
  fresh basil

¹/₂ teaspoon salt
¹/₈ teaspoon pepper
1 cup torn fresh spinach

In slow-cooker, combine all ingredients. Cover and
cook on LOW 10 to 11 hours or until beans are
tender. Makes about 8 servings.

1 serving contains:

Cal	Prot	Carb	Fat	Chol	Sodium
307	25g	36g	8g	38mg	322mg

Garbanzo beans are also known as chick peas, cei,
or chana dol. *They're a staple in Middle Eastern,
European and Oriental diets.*

BASIC CHICKEN STOCK

*You can freeze this flavorful stock in 1- or 2-cup
containers for later use in casseroles or soup.*

3 lbs. chicken necks,
    backs or wings
2 carrots, peeled, finely
    chopped
2 leeks, finely chopped
2 stalks celery with
    leaves, finely
    chopped

5 or 6 whole black
    peppercorns
¼ cup loosely packed
    watercress
1 teaspoon fresh
    tarragon leaves
1 teaspoon salt
2 quarts water

Arrange chicken in single layer in shallow roasting
pan. Bake in 325F (165C) oven about 1 hour or until
brown, turning pieces as they brown. Transfer
browned chicken to slow-cooker. Add remaining
ingredients. Cover and cook on LOW 10 to 12 hours
or until vegetables are very tender. Strain broth
through fine sieve; discard vegetables and chicken.
Refrigerate stock until cold; remove fat, if desired.
Makes about 7 cups.

1 cup contains:

Cal	Prot	Carb	Fat	Chol	Sodium
39	5g	1g	1g	1mg	305mg

If watercress is not available use fresh parsley.

BEEF STOCK

*Use bones with a small amount of meat on them to
ensure a better beef flavor.*

3 lbs. beef bones
2 carrots, peeled, finely
  chopped
1 medium onion,
  chopped
2 stalks celery with
  leaves, finely
  chopped

2 bay leaves
1 teaspoon fresh thyme
  leaves
5 or 6 black
  peppercorns
1/2 teaspoon salt
2 quarts water

Arrange single layer of bones in shallow roasting pan.
Bake in 325F (165C) oven about 1 hour or until
brown, turning bones as they brown. Transfer
browned bones to slow-cooker. Add remaining
ingredients. Cover and cook on LOW 10 to 12 hours
or until vegetables are very tender. Strain broth
through fine strainer; discard herbs, vegetables, bones

and meat. Refrigerate stock until cold; remove fat, if
desired. Makes about 7 cups.

1 cup contains:

Cal	Prot	Carb	Fat	Chol	Sodium
16	3g	0	1g	1mg	152mg

*Roasting the bones beforehand gives the stock a rich
deep color and better flavor.*

VEGETARIAN STOCK

*Add a cup or two of this basic stock to intensify
flavors of a vegetable sauce.*

3 carrots, peeled, finely
  chopped

1 large leek, finely
  chopped
2 stalks celery with

leaves, finely
chopped
2 parsnips, peeled,
finely chopped
1/2 cup loosely packed
parsley leaves
1/4 cup loosely packed
watercress leaves

6 mushrooms, chopped
2 quarts water
1/2 teaspoon salt
1/2 teaspoon black
peppercorns

In slow-cooker, combine all ingredients. Cover and
cook on LOW 10 to 12 hours or until vegetables are
very tender. Strain broth through a fine strainer;
discard vegetables. Makes about 7 cups.

1 cup contains:

Cal	Prot	Carb	Fat	Chol	Sodium
34	1g	7g	0	0	72mg

*To prevent bubbling over, do not fill slow-cooker to
the brim.*

SLOW-COOKER ENTERTAINING

While you're busy with last-minute chores before entertaining, your slow-cooker continues cooking unattended. It could be cooking a new hot appetizer or an exciting main dish. Or it will keep foods warm that you've cooked in the microwave or on the stovetop. You can rest assured that the food will be just as warm for the last guest as it was for the first.

The crockery-cooker makes an excellent serving container for hot punch or cider during a holiday open house or for Halloween revelers.

It's possible to prepare festive, long-cooking fare the day before a party. Refrigerate the food overnight; then reheat it and keep it in a warm (on LOW) slow-cooker throughout a buffet or cocktail party.

**Sicilian Hens on Fettuccine, page 109**
**Sorrento Chicken, page 114**
**Turkey Marsala with Vegetables, page 105**

Entertaining is a pleasure when your slow-cooker is working for you. Enjoy a delicious Italian dinner with a minimum of effort. Prepare the salad the day before and serve it well chilled. The Sicilian Hens on Fettuccine are sure to please family and guests alike.

MENU

Antipasto Bean Salad, page 180
Sicilian Hens on Fettuccine, page 109
Steamed Broccoli
Garlic Bread
Strawberries and Cantaloupe

TURKEY MARSALA
WITH VEGETABLES

If your slow-cooker is large enough to accommodate a whole turkey breast, consider it for a larger get-together.

3 large carrots, peeled, julienned

2 leeks, washed, julienned

$^{1}/_{2}$ (about 3 lbs.) turkey breast, skinned

2 tablespoons melted margarine or butter

12 mushrooms, sliced

$^{1}/_{2}$ teaspoon salt

$^{1}/_{8}$ teaspoon pepper

2 tablespoons chopped fresh parsley

$^{3}/_{4}$ cup chicken broth or bouillon

$^{1}/_{2}$ cup Marsala or dry sherry

2 tablespoons cornstarch

2 tablespoons cold water

Place carrots and leeks in slow-cooker. Brush turkey breast with melted margarine or butter. Arrange turkey, then mushrooms over vegetables. Sprinkle with salt, pepper and parsley. Pour broth or bouillon and wine over all. Cover and cook on LOW 6 to 7 hours. Remove turkey and vegetables with slotted spoon; cover and keep warm. Turn pot on HIGH. Dissolve cornstarch in water. Stir into juices in pot. Cover and cook on HIGH 15 to 20 minutes or until thickened, stirring occasionally. Slice turkey; arrange on center of platter with vegetables around edges. Serve with Marsala sauce. Makes 5 or 6 servings.

1 serving contains:

Cal	Prot	Carb	Fat	Chol	Sodium
287	36g	13g	7g	79mg	321mg

PEPPERCORN PORK

When you purchase the pork roast, consider the size of your slow-cooker. Some large roasts do not fit into a 3¹/₂ quart pot.

2 tablespoons drained
   green peppercorns
3 tablespoons sweet-hot
   mustard
1 teaspoon horseradish
¹/₂ teaspoon grated
   lemon peel
¹/₄ teaspoon salt
3¹/₂ to 4 lbs. lean pork
   roast

1 cup apple cider

¹/₄ cup cold water
3 tablespoons
   cornstarch
1 apple, cored, cut into
   thin wedges

In small bowl, combine peppercorns, mustard, horseradish, lemon peel and salt. Spread on top and sides of pork roast. Place metal rack in bottom of slow-cooker; pour in cider. Place coated pork roast on rack in slow-cooker. Cover and cook on LOW 9 to 10 hours. Then turn slow-cooker on HIGH. Remove pork and rack; cover and keep warm. In small bowl, combine water and cornstarch; stir until smooth. Add to drippings in pot. Cook on HIGH 20 to 30 minutes or until thickened, stirring occasionally. Slice roast; garnish with apple wedges. Serve pork with sauce. Makes 6 to 8 servings.

1 serving contains:

Cal	Prot	Carb	Fat	Chol	Sodium
396	44g	8g	20g	139mg	240mg

FLANK STEAK PINWHEELS

Smaller slow-cookers (3½- or 4-quart) are the ideal size for this recipe.

1 (about 1½-lbs.) beef
  flank steak
2 tablespoons chutney
1 tablespoon soy sauce
1 tablespoon white
  wine vinegar
1 tablespoon vegetable
  oil

1 garlic clove, crushed
¼ teaspoon salt
⅛ teaspoon pepper

Cooked rice or noodles

Trim all fat off flank steak; cut into 8 crosswise strips.
Roll up; secure with small wooden pick. Place in
bottom of slow-cooker. In small bowl, combine
chutney, soy sauce, vinegar, oil, garlic, salt and
pepper. Spoon over steak pinwheels. Cover and cook
on LOW about 6 hours or until tender. Remove
wooden picks. Serve pinwheels and the meat juices
over cooked rice or noodles. Makes 8 steak pinwheels.

1 pinwheel contains:

Cal	Prot	Carb	Fat	Chol	Sodium
150	17g	1g	8g	43mg	281mg

SICILIAN HENS
ON FETTUCCINE

For a change of pace, impress your guests with this dish with an Italian accent.

¹/₄ cup toasted sliced
  almonds
3 tablespoons drained
  capers
3 tablespoons chopped
  fresh parsley
1 garlic clove, chopped
¹/₂ teaspoon paprika
2 teaspoons olive or
  vegetable oil

¹/₂ teaspoon salt
¹/₈ teaspoon pepper
2 Cornish hens, thawed,
  halved

Cooked fettuccine
Chopped ripe olives

In food processor fitted with metal blade, combine almonds, capers, parsley, garlic, paprika, oil, salt and pepper. Process until finely chopped but not puréed. Pat mixture on all sides of Cornish hens. Place on rack in slow-cooker. If all hens do not fit on rack, place 2 halves on rack; lightly cover with heavy-duty foil. Arrange remaining halves on top of foil. Cover and cook on LOW 7 to 8 hours. Serve on fettuccine; sprinkle with chopped ripe olives. Makes 4 servings.

1 serving contains:

Cal	Prot	Carb	Fat	Chol	Sodium
234	32g	1g	11g	94mg	484mg

Capers are the pickled flower buds of Mediterranean shrubs; they vary in size and color.

HERB-STUFFED TURKEY BREAST

Extra sprigs of fresh thyme and parsley make attractive garnishes for cooked turkey slices.

1 (2¼- to 2½-lbs.) half
   turkey breast, boned,
   with skin

1 tablespoon Dijon-style
   mustard
6 thin slices (about

¹/₂ lb.) Canadian
bacon
1 tablespoon chopped
    fresh thyme
1 tablespoon chopped
    fresh parsley

¹/₄ teaspoon salt
¹/₈ teaspoon pepper

1 tablespoon cornstarch
¹/₄ cup dry white wine

Place turkey breast skin-side down. Spread cut
surfaces with mustard; top with Canadian bacon,
thyme and parsley. Fold long sides of breast over
stuffing so they overlap slightly. Skewer or tie to hold
sides together. Sprinkle with salt and pepper. Place
skin-side up on rack in slow-cooker. Cover and cook
on LOW about 6 hours. Remove turkey and rack from
pot; let juices remain. Keep covered and warm. Turn
pot on HIGH. Dissolve cornstarch in wine. Stir into
drippings in pot. Cover and cook on HIGH 20 to 30
minutes or until thickened, stirring occasionally.
Remove skewer or tie from turkey. Slice turkey
crosswise into ³/₈- or ¹/₂-inch slices. Spoon wine sauce
over slices. Makes 6 to 8 servings.

1 serving contains:

Cal	Prot	Carb	Fat	Chol	Sodium
241	43g	1g	6g	99mg	443mg

*If fresh herbs are not available, substitute 1 teaspoon
dried for each tablespoon fresh.*

ITALIAN ROLL-UPS

This will enhance your reputation as a hostess.

¹/₄ cup pine nuts, coarsely chopped

1 garlic clove, minced

2 tablespoons chopped fresh parsley

2 tablespoons chopped fresh basil

1 tablespoon olive or vegetable oil

¹/₄ teaspoon salt

¹/₈ teaspoon pepper

1¹/₂ lbs. boneless round steak, about ¹/₂-inch thick

6 slices proscuitto, well trimmed

1 cup beef broth or bouillon

1 oz. dried porcini or shitake mushrooms

¹/₂ cup dry red wine

2 tablespoons cornstarch

¹/₄ cup cold water

Pine nuts

In small bowl, combine ¹/₄ cup chopped pine nuts, garlic, parsley, basil, oil, salt and pepper. Remove most of fat from steak. Cut into 6 pieces about 3″ × 4″. Pound to about ¹/₄-inch thickness or 4″ × 6″. Place a slice of proscuitto on each slice of pounded round steak. Spoon about 1 tablespoon herb mixture

on each. Roll up like a jelly roll. Tie with string. Place
on bottom of slow-cooker. Heat broth or bouillon to
boiling. Pour over dried mushrooms. Add to cooker.
Pour in wine. Cover; cook on LOW 6 to 7 hours.
Remove meat; cover and keep warm. Turn pot on
HIGH. Dissolve cornstarch in water. Stir into liquid in
pot. Cover; cook on HIGH 15 to 20 minutes or until
thickened. Spoon over roll-ups. Sprinkle with
additional pine nuts. Makes 6 servings.

1 serving contains:

Cal	Prot	Carb	Fat	Chol	Sodium
326	36g	7g	15g	101mg	395mg

SORRENTO CHICKEN

To make a very smooth sauce, process thickened broth in food processor just before spooning it over chicken.

1 tablespoon Dijon-style mustard

¹/₂ teaspoon chopped fresh tarragon

1 teaspoon minced fresh chives

¹/₄ teaspoon salt

¹/₈ teaspoon pepper

6 chicken breast halves, boned, skinned

1¹/₂ oz. proscuitto, cut into 6 (1″ × 9″) strips

1 cup fresh pearl onions, peeled

¹/₂ cup dry white wine

¹/₂ cup chicken broth or bouillon

1 cup seasoned croutons

Combine mustard, tarragon, chives, salt and pepper. Spread on chicken breasts. Wrap strip of proscuitto around each. Place rack in bottom of slow-cooker. Top with wrapped chicken and onions. Combine wine and chicken broth or bouillon; pour over chicken. Cover and cook on LOW 5 to 6 hours or until chicken is tender. Remove chicken and rack; cover and keep warm. Turn pot on HIGH. Pulverize croutons in food processor until they look like brown sugar. Stir into broth mixture. Cover and cook on HIGH 15 to 20 minutes or until thickened. Spoon over cooked chicken breasts. Makes 6 servings.

1 serving contains:

Cal	Prot	Carb	Fat	Chol	Sodium
124	17g	5g	2g	41mg	315mg

MEDITERRANEAN RATATOUILLE

Keep warm in a slow-cooker during a party. Let guests dip pita wedges into it. A versatile dish that can serve as a main dish, side dish or appetizer.

1 large eggplant, peeled, cubed
2 tomatoes, peeled, seeded, cubed
3 zucchini, cubed
1 small onion, chopped
1 yellow bell pepper, cubed
1/4 cup vegetable oil
1 garlic clove, crushed

1/4 cup chopped fresh cilantro leaves
2 tablespoons chopped fresh basil
1/2 teaspoon salt
1/4 teaspoon pepper

Pita bread, cut into wedges

Combine eggplant, tomatoes, zucchini, onion and bell pepper in slow-cooker. In small bowl, combine oil, garlic, cilantro, basil, salt and pepper. Add to vegetables in pot. Cover and cook on LOW 7 to 8 hours or until vegetables are tender. Use as a hearty vegetable dip or appetizer with pita bread. Makes 6 to 8 servings as a main dish; 20 to 25 as a dip.

1 serving contains:

Cal	Prot	Carb	Fat	Chol	Sodium
91	1g	7g	7g	0	140mg

BLACK BEAN-JALAPEÑO MOUSSE

If your digestive system is jalapeño-friendly, use 2 jalapeño peppers. An excellent brunch dish that is tasty with grilled chicken and fresh fruit.

6 slices bacon, chopped
1 lb. dried black beans, rinsed
1 jalapeño pepper, seeded, chopped
1/2 teaspoon salt
1/4 teaspoon pepper
2 (10 1/2-oz.) cans beef broth
1 teaspoon instant beef bouillon
1 cup red wine vinegar
1 cup dry red wine
1 cup water
8 oz. smoked ham, diced

1 cup chopped fresh cilantro
1 large onion, chopped
2 envelopes unflavored gelatin
1/3 cup cold water

Goat Cheese Topping:
5 oz. goat cheese
1/4 cup dairy sour cream
1/3 cup nonfat milk
2 green onions, chopped

Stuffed green olives and fresh cilantro sprigs

Sauté bacon until crisp, drain; set aside. Spray 8-inch springform pan with no-stick cooking spray; set aside. Rinse beans; drain. Pour beans into slow-cooker. Top with jalapeño pepper, salt and pepper. In 3- or 4-quart saucepan, combine beef broth, bouillon, vinegar, wine, 1 cup water, ham, chopped cilantro, onion and bacon. Cover and cook on medium-high until mixture boils. Pour into slow-cooker; stir. Cover and cook on HIGH 6 hours or until beans are tender. When beans are tender, sprinkle gelatin over ⅓ cup water. When softened, stir into hot beans. Purée half of bean mixture at a time. Pour purée into springform pan; cover and refrigerate.

Goat Cheese Topping: Combine cheese, sour cream, milk and green onions; stir until well blended. Cover and refrigerate until serving time. To serve, remove side of springform pan; cut into wedges. Top with Cheese Topping; garnish with olives and cilantro, if desired. Makes 8 or 10 servings.

1 serving contains:

Cal	Prot	Carb	Fat	Chol	Sodium
272	21g	25g	9g	35mg	833mg

PERSIMMON PUDDING

The bright orange, fig-shaped Hachiya persimmon should be very soft; the reddish-orange, tomato-shaped Fuyu can be slightly firm.

1 1/2 cups all-purpose
   flour
1 cup sugar
1 teaspoon baking
   powder
1 teaspoon baking soda
1 teaspoon cinnamon
1/4 teaspoon nutmeg
2 persimmons
1 tablespoon lemon
   juice
1/3 cup milk
1 egg
2 tablespoons honey
1/4 cup melted
   margarine or butter

1/2 cup chopped raisins
1/4 cup chopped pecans

Hot Citrus Sauce:
2 tablespoons
   cornstarch
1/2 cup sugar
1/2 cup water
1/2 cup orange juice
2 tablespoons margarine
1/4 teaspoon grated
   lemon peel
3 tablespoons lemon
   juice

Grease 6- or 8-cup heat-proof mold. In large bowl,
combine flour, sugar, baking powder, soda, cinnamon
and nutmeg; set aside. Cut persimmons in half; scoop
out pulp. Purée lemon juice and pulp in blender or
food processor fitted with metal blade. Add milk, egg,
honey and margarine; process until well blended. Stir
liquid into flour mixture. Add raisins and nuts. Spoon
into mold; cover. Place on rack in slow-cooker. Pour
in boiling water until it comes halfway up sides of
mold. Cover and steam on HIGH 3 hours. Loosen
sides by inserting a knife between pudding and sides
of mold. Invert on a platter. Serve with Hot Citrus
Sauce. Makes 6 to 8 servings.

Hot Citrus Sauce: In small saucepan, combine
cornstarch and sugar. Add water and orange juice; stir
until smooth. Stir over medium-low heat until
thickened and translucent. Add margarine; stir until
melted. Remove from heat. Stir in lemon peel and
juice. Makes about 1½ cups.

1 serving with sauce contains:

Cal	Prot	Carb	Fat	Chol	Sodium
414	5g	80g	10g	28mg	266

HOLIDAY CRAN-APPLE SAUCE

A very versatile dish! It's equally good as an accompaniment to poultry, dessert or breakfast fruit.

1 cup fresh cranberries
8 apples, peeled, cored,
   chopped
½ cup sugar

1 stick cinnamon,
   halved crosswise
6 whole cloves

Ground nutmeg

Combine cranberries, apples and sugar in slow-cooker. Place cinnamon and cloves in center of a 6-inch square of cheesecloth. Pull up around sides; tie to form pouch. Place in pot. Cover and cook on LOW 4 to 5 hours or until cranberries and apples are very soft. Remove spice bag. Purée hot fruit in blender or food processor fitted with metal blade. Sprinkle with nutmeg. Makes about 3½ cups.

1 tablespoon contains:

Cal	Prot	Carb	Fat	Chol	Sodium
18	0	5g	0	0	0

PUNCH-OF-GOLD

The easiest punch you've ever made; keep it hot in the slow-cooker for guests to help themselves.

2 (12-oz.) cans apricot
   nectar
1 quart orange juice
1/4 cup orange liqueur
2 (12-oz.) cans mango
   nectar

3 pieces crystallized
   ginger, halved
2 cinnamon sticks

Fresh mint leaves

In slow-cooker, combine all ingredients except mint leaves. Cover; cook on LOW 4 or 5 hours. With slotted spoon, remove ginger and cinnamon sticks. Serve in punch cups or coffee mugs; garnish with mint leaves. Makes 15 to 18 servings.

1 serving contains:

Cal	Prot	Carb	Fat	Chol	Sodium
82	1g	18g	0	0	3mg

Keep slow-cooker on LOW to keep punch warm during the evening; this is ideal for buffet serving.

HONEY-BUTTERED
CRANBERRY CIDER

Try this bright, vibrantly flavored beverage. The slow-cooker keeps it hot until guests are ready for it.

1 (48-oz.) bottle
cranberry juice
cocktail
1 quart apple juice or
cider
4 thin strips orange
peel, about 2 inches
long

$^1/_3$ cup margarine or
butter
$^1/_4$ cup honey
$^1/_2$ teaspoon ground
coriander

In slow-cooker, combine cranberry juice, apple juice or cider and orange peel. Cover and heat on LOW 5 to 7 hours. Just before serving, melt margarine or butter, honey and coriander in small saucepan or in microwave. Spoon slightly more than $^1/_2$ tablespoon honey-margarine mixture in mug or heat-proof cup; add about $^3/_4$ cup hot cranberry mixture. Serve immediately. Makes 12 to 15 servings.

1 serving contains:

Cal	Prot	Carb	Fat	Chol	Sodium
127	0	25g	3g	0	54mg

FIESTA BLACK-BEAN DIP

Guests who enjoy more spicy foods will enjoy adding a bit of fresh or bottled salsa on each chip.

1 cup dried black beans, rinsed

1 quart water

1 onion, chopped

1 garlic clove, crushed

¹/₄ cup chopped fresh cilantro

¹/₄ teaspoon salt

1 fresh jalapeño pepper, seeded, chopped

¹/₄ lb. salt pork, coarsely chopped

2 or 3 oz. goat cheese, crumbled

Fresh cilantro leaves for garnish

Taco or tortilla chips

Salsa, optional

In slow-cooker, combine dried beans, water, onion, garlic, ¼ cup chopped cilantro, salt, jalapeño pepper and salt pork. Cover and cook on LOW 9 to 10 hours or until beans are soft. Drain; discard water. In blender or food processor fitted with metal blade, process drained bean mixture until almost smooth. Spoon into serving bowl. Sprinkle cheese and fresh cilantro leaves over top. Dip chips into bean mixture. Top with salsa, if desired. Makes about 2½ cups.

1 tablespoon contains:

Cal	Prot	Carb	Fat	Chol	Sodium
24	1g	2g	1g	2mg	55mg

ROUND-THE-WORLD FLAVORS

It's fun to borrow traditional flavors from other parts of the world. Good cooks in Europe have been "slow-cooking" for centuries. These early versions of slow-cookers were not electric, but heavy iron pots that simmered on the back of the stove or on the edge of a fireplace.

Our round-the-world recipes are not designed to be authentic replicas of ethnic or regional dishes. Instead we used favorite flavor combinations that have been traditional for generations. Then we adapted them for use in slow-cooking.

Taste-of-Thai Chicken Salad, page 131
Tortilla Stack, page 147
Turkey Moussaka in Taco Shell, page 144

France is famous for its fine food and unique flavor combinations. Savor the blend of spices in the classic Cassoulet, The Crockery Way. Sliced fresh mushrooms with a simple vinaigrette dressing makes an ideal salad. Crusty French bread complements the superb entrée.

MENU

Cassoulet, The Crockery Way, page 152
Fresh Mushroom Salad
French Bread
Apple Tart

SLOW-COOKER TAMALE PIE

When serving, be sure to include part of cornmeal lining in addition to meat mixture in the center.

2 cups chicken broth or bouillon
1 cup yellow cornmeal
1 tablespoon chopped fresh cilantro
1/2 lb. pork sausage
1 lb. beef stew meat, cut into 1/2-inch cubes
1 onion, chopped
1/2 cup finely chopped celery
1 mild green chile

pepper, seeded, chopped
1/2 cup chopped sun-dried tomatoes
1 (8-oz.) can whole-kernel corn, drained
1 (2 1/2-oz.) can sliced ripe olives, drained
1/2 teaspoon salt
1/8 teaspoon pepper
Whole or halved pitted ripe olives, optional

Bring broth or bouillon to boil in medium saucepan. Stirring constantly, slowly add cornmeal. Simmer mixture 5 minutes, stirring occasionally. Stir in cilantro. Using a greased spatula, spread cornmeal mixture on bottom and about 2 inches up sides of slow-cooker. In large bowl, combine sausage, stew meat, onion, celery, chile pepper, sun-dried tomatoes, corn, sliced olives, salt and pepper. Carefully spoon into center of cornmeal-lined pot. Cover and cook on LOW 7 to 8 hours. Garnish with ripe olives, if desired. Makes 6 or 7 servings. Do not remove cover during cooking because heat escapes quickly.

1 serving contains:

Cal	Prot	Carb	Fat	Chol	Sodium
372	24g	24g	20g	69mg	566mg

AEGEAN LAMB AND EGGPLANT ON FETTUCCINE

Popular flavor combination of lamb and eggplant plus intriguing accents of sun-dried tomatoes and Feta cheese.

1 small eggplant, peeled, cut into 1-inch cubes
1 small onion, chopped
¼ cup sun-dried tomatoes in oil, chopped
¼ teaspoon dried red-pepper flakes
1 tablespoon balsamic vinegar

¼ teaspoon salt
1 tablespoon chopped fresh basil
1 lb. lamb stew meat, cut into 2″ × ½″ strips

Cooked fettuccine
Feta cheese, crumbled
Fresh basil leaves

In slow-cooker, combine eggplant, onion, sun-dried tomatoes, red-pepper flakes, vinegar, salt, basil and lamb. Cover; cook on LOW 5 to 6 hours or until lamb is tender. Remove from cooker; spoon over cooked fettuccine. Top with crumbled feta cheese. Garnish with fresh basil leaves. Makes 4 to 5 servings.

1 serving contains:

Cal	Prot	Carb	Fat	Chol	Sodium
195	19g	4g	11g	61mg	156mg

TASTE-OF-THAI CHICKEN SALAD

Avoid the boning process by substituting 6 boneless chicken breast halves for the whole fryer.

1 (2½- to 3-lbs.) chicken
1 cup chicken broth
½ teaspoon dry red-pepper flakes
½ teaspoon seasoned salt
1 tablespoon chopped fresh chives

1 cup snow peas
1 (8-oz.) can sliced water chestnuts, drained
1 red bell pepper, thinly sliced

¼ cup vegetable oil
1 tablespoon sesame oil
1 tablespoon lime juice
2 tablespoons white wine vinegar
1 tablespoon soy sauce
2 teaspoons finely chopped fresh ginger root
Tabasco® sauce
1 garlic clove, crushed
1 orange, peeled, sliced
¼ cup salted peanuts

Cut chicken in pieces; place in slow-cooker. In small bowl, combine broth, red-pepper flakes, seasoned salt and chives. Pour over chicken. Cover and cook on LOW 4 to 5 hours or until chicken is done. Cool; remove meat from bones. Cut meat into bite-size pieces. Discard bones; use broth for soup or stew. Blanch snow peas; cool. In large bowl, combine chicken, snow peas, water chestnuts and bell pepper. In small bowl, combine oils, lime juice, vinegar, soy sauce, ginger root, 3 or 4 dashes of Tabasco® and garlic. Add to chicken mixture; toss. Top with orange slices and sprinkle with chopped peanuts just before serving. Makes 5 or 6 servings.

1 serving contains:

Cal	Prot	Carb	Fat	Chol	Sodium
355	30g	12g	21g	79mg	446mg

Thai foods are often fragrant with spicy surprises and are always beautifully presented.

MINESTRONE NAPOLI

A satisfying and delicious soup that is hearty enough to be used as a main dish.

3 large tomatoes,
    peeled, seeded,
    chopped
1 bunch green onions,
    chopped
2 medium carrots,
    peeled, chopped
1/4 cup chopped fresh
    parsley
1 garlic clove, crushed
2 tablespoons chopped
    fresh basil leaves
1 (15-oz.) can red
    kidney beans, drained
2 zucchini, sliced

2 cups shredded
    cabbage
1/2 teaspoon chopped
    fresh oregano
1/2 teaspoon salt
1/8 teaspoon pepper
5 cups beef broth or
    bouillon
1/4 cup dry red wine

2 cups cooked small
    elbow pasta
1/4 cup grated Parmesan
    cheese, optional

In slow-cooker, combine tomatoes, green onions, carrots, parsley, garlic, basil, kidney beans, zucchini, cabbage, oregano, salt, pepper, broth and wine. Cover and cook on LOW 8 to 9 hours. Stir in cooked pasta. Sprinkle with cheese, if desired. Makes 10 cups.

1 cup contains:

Cal	Prot	Carb	Fat	Chol	Sodium
113	6g	21g	1g	0	265mg

GREEK ISLES PITA POCKETS

At your next party, keep the cooked shredded meat in your slow-cooker; guests will enjoy assembling everything.

1½ lbs. lamb stew meat, cut into 1-inch cubes
¾ lb. banana squash, peeled, cut into 1-inch cubes
1 medium red onion, diced
½ cup sliced celery
½ teaspoon salt
1 jalapeño pepper, seeded, minced
1 cube chicken bouillon, crushed or 1 teaspoon bouillon granules

1 garlic clove, crushed
⅛ teaspoon ground cumin
⅛ teaspoon ground coriander

8 to 10 pita bread rounds
8 to 10 lettuce leaves
¼ cup (1 oz.) feta cheese, crumbled
¼ cup plain yogurt

In slow-cooker, combine lamb, squash, onion, celery, salt, jalapeño pepper, bouillon, garlic, cumin and coriander. Cover and cook on LOW 8 to 9 hours or until meat is very tender. Strain mixture. Reserve about ¼ cup broth; use remaining broth for soup or stew, if desired. Process drained cooked-meat mixture with reserved ¼ cup broth in food processor until shredded. Cut about 1 inch off top of each pita round. Insert lettuce leaf into each. Spoon in meat mixture. Top with cheese and yogurt. Makes 8 to 10 servings.

1 serving contains:

Cal	Prot	Carb	Fat	Chol	Sodium
309	24g	38g	7g	54mg	654mg

Use caution when working with jalapeño or chile peppers; they can irritate your skin. Wear rubber gloves for protection if you have sensitive skin.

NEAPOLITAN TOSTADA

Halve each pita round horizontally to form 2 shell-like rounds; then toast just before serving.

³/₄ lb. ground turkey

1 eggplant, cubed

1 cup fresh or canned salsa

1 (6-oz.) can tomato paste

¹/₄ cup chopped fresh parsley

1 tablespoon chili powder

1 teaspoon ground cumin

1 teaspoon dried
  oregano
1 (10-oz.) pkg. frozen
  corn, thawed

4 pita rounds, halved,
  toasted

¹/₂ cup plain lowfat
  yogurt
2 cups shredded lettuce
¹/₂ cup sliced ripe olives
¹/₂ cup shredded cheese,
  optional

Combine turkey, eggplant, salsa, tomato paste, parsley,
chili powder, cumin, oregano and corn in slow-
cooker. Cover and cook on LOW 5 to 6 hours. Stir
with a fork to break up large chunks of turkey. Spoon
about ³/₄ cup cooked turkey mixture on each pita half.
Top with yogurt, lettuce, olives and cheese, if desired.
Makes 8 servings.

1 serving contains:

Cal	Prot	Carb	Fat	Chol	Sodium
256	16g	34g	8g	26mg	328mg

OLD WORLD GOULASH

Flavors borrowed from our European heritage create this hearty dish.

1½ lbs. boneless beef chuck, cut into 1-inch cubes
1 onion, sliced
2 teaspoons paprika
¼ teaspoon salt
⅛ teaspoon pepper
½ cup beef broth or bouillon
2 medium potatoes, peeled, shredded

1 (14-oz.) can sauerkraut, drained
1 tablespoon brown sugar
¼ teaspoon caraway seeds
½ cup plain lowfat yogurt or dairy sour cream

In slow-cooker, combine beef and onion. Sprinkle with paprika, salt and pepper. Pour broth or bouillon over all. Top with shredded potatoes, sauerkraut, brown sugar and caraway seeds. Cover and cook on LOW 8 to 9 hours. Turn off heat; stir in yogurt or sour cream. Makes 6 to 7 servings.

1 serving contains:

Cal	Prot	Carb	Fat	Chol	Sodium
265	25g	14g	12g	78mg	517

PROVENÇALE SMOKED SAUSAGE RATATOUILLE

This recipe is a cross between a stew and a soup; it contains our favorite flavors of southern France.

1 eggplant, peeled, cut into ½-inch cubes
3 zucchini, cut into ½-inch slices
1 medium onion, sliced
2 medium tomatoes
1 large green bell pepper
1 large yellow bell pepper

1 jalapeño pepper
1 tablespoon chopped fresh basil
¼ teaspoon salt
1 tablespoon minced parsley
½ lb. smoked link sausage, thinly sliced
2 cups chicken broth or bouillon

Combine eggplant, zucchini and onion in slow-cooker. With sharp knife, make an X in skin at smooth end of tomatoes. Drop in boiling water for about 15 seconds; pull off skin. Halve and remove tomato and bell pepper seeds. Cut tomatoes and bell peppers in 1/2-inch pieces; seed and finely chop jalapeño pepper. Add tomatoes, peppers, basil, salt, parsley, smoked sausage and broth or bouillon to slow-cooker. Stir; cover and cook on LOW 4 to 6 hours. Makes 7 to 8 servings.

1 serving contains:

Cal	Prot	Carb	Fat	Chol	Sodium
138	6g	8g	9g	20mg	357mg

BRAZILIAN FEIJOADA

Not quite as elaborate as the traditional dish of Brazil but with similar flavors.

1 lb. dried black beans, rinsed

1 medium onion, chopped

1 garlic clove, crushed

2 tomatoes, peeled, seeded, chopped

1 tablespoon chopped jalapeño pepper

1 tablespoon chopped
fresh parsley

¼ lb. Canadian bacon in
one piece

3 or 4 oz. beef jerky,
cut each into 12ths

1 lb. smoked sausage

links, cut each into
3rds

2 quarts water

2 oranges, peeled, thinly
sliced

Cooked rice

In 5-quart slow-cooker, combine beans, onion, garlic,
tomatoes, jalapeño pepper and parsley. Top with
Canadian bacon, jerky and sausage. Pour water over
all. Cover and cook on LOW 10 to 12 hours or until
beans are tender. With slotted spoon, remove meat
from slow-cooker. Scoop out about 3 cups beans with
liquid. In blender or food processor fitted with metal
blade, process these beans until almost smooth. Drain
remaining beans; discard liquid. Combine puréed
beans with drained beans. Spoon all beans on large
platter. Slice Canadian bacon and sausage. Arrange
jerky and sliced meat around side of platter. Serve
with sliced oranges and cooked rice. Makes 10 to 12
servings.

1 serving contains:

Cal	Prot	Carb	Fat	Chol	Sodium
276	17g	23g	13g	39mg	518mg

NEW-STYLE POZOLE

A delicious potpourri of flavors with overtones of the traditional recipe.

1 lb. boneless pork
   shoulder, cubed
1 lb. chicken thighs
2 slices bacon, chopped
1 small onion, chopped
1/2 teaspoon salt
1 cup chicken broth or
   bouillon

1 garlic clove, crushed
1 teaspoon chili powder
2 (16-oz.) cans hominy,
   drained
1/4 teaspoon crushed
   dried red-pepper
   flakes

Paprika

In slow-cooker, combine all ingredients except paprika. Cover and cook on LOW 6 to 7 hours or until meat is tender. With slotted spoon, remove chicken from pot; remove and discard bones. Cut chicken into slivers; return to pot. Refrigerate. When cold, skim and remove fat. Just before serving, heat in microwave or on stovetop. Sprinkle with paprika. Makes 8 to 10 servings.

1 serving contains:

Cal	Prot	Carb	Fat	Chol	Sodium
202	18g	12g	8g	58mg	207mg

In New Mexico, traditional pozole is served on Christmas Eve. Serve with crusty French bread or tortillas.

SLOW-POKE JAMBALAYA

Flavors that are typical of this classic Creole dish have plenty of time to mingle in the slow-cooker.

1 large red or green bell pepper, seeded, chopped
1 large onion, chopped
2 medium tomatoes, chopped
1 cup chopped celery
1 garlic clove, crushed
2 tablespoons minced fresh parsley
2 teaspoons chopped fresh thyme leaves
2 teaspoons chopped fresh oregano leaves
1/8 teaspoon cayenne
1/2 teaspoon salt

2 cups beef broth or
   bouillon
4 oz. smoked sausage,
   chopped
8 oz. chicken breast,
   skinned, boned,
   chopped

½ lb. cooked, shelled
   medium shrimp,
   halved lengthwise
1 cup cooked rice

In slow-cooker, combine all ingredients except shrimp
and rice. Cover and cook on LOW 9 to 10 hours. Turn
slow-cooker on HIGH; add cooked shrimp and cooked
rice. Cover; cook on HIGH 20 to 30 minutes. Makes 7
to 8 servings.

1 serving contains:

Cal	Prot	Carb	Fat	Chol	Sodium
166	18g	9g	6g	90mg	369mg

TURKEY MOUSSAKA
IN TACO SHELL

_Make your own taco shells from corn tortillas or buy
a package of ready-made ones; heat in microwave or
oven._

³/₄ lb. ground turkey
1 medium onion,
  chopped
4 mushrooms, sliced
1 garlic clove, crushed
1 (6-oz.) can tomato
  paste
¹/₂ cup dry white wine
1 tablespoon chopped
  parsley
¹/₂ teaspoon salt
1 teaspoon pickling
  spices
4 whole peppercorns

Yogurt Cream Sauce:
1 tablespoon margarine
  or butter
1 tablespoon all-purpose
  flour
¹/₈ teaspoon salt
¹/₃ cup milk
1 egg, beaten slightly
¹/₂ cup unflavored
  yogurt
¹/₁₆ teaspoon ground
  nutmeg

8 taco shells

In slow-cooker, combine turkey, onion, mushrooms,
garlic, tomato paste, wine, parsley and salt. Tie
pickling spices and peppercorns in cheesecloth bag or
place them in a tea ball. Add to pot; cover and cook
on LOW about 5 hours. Remove spice bag. Prepare
Yogurt Cream Sauce. Spoon about ¹/₄ cup moussaka
into each taco shell. Top with Yogurt Cream Sauce.
Makes 8 tacos.

Yogurt Cream Sauce: In small saucepan or microwave,
melt margarine or butter; stir in flour and salt.
Gradually add milk. Cook and stir over low heat until

thickened. Remove from heat. In small bowl, combine egg, yogurt and nutmeg. Stir into hot mixture in pan. Return to heat. Cook and stir over low heat 1 minute. Serve over moussaka.

1 taco contains:

Cal	Prot	Carb	Fat	Chol	Sodium
199	12g	17g	9g	50mg	310mg

COQ AU VIN

Slow-cooker version of classic French dish of chicken with wine.

1 (2¹/₂- to 3-lb.) chicken,
   cut up
2 slices bacon, cooked,
   drained, chopped

4 shallots, peeled, sliced
1 garlic clove, crushed
1 tablespoon chopped
   fresh parsley

1 bay leaf
1/2 teaspoon chopped
   fresh thyme
1/4 teaspoon salt
1/8 teaspoon pepper
15 small white boiling
   onions
10 mushrooms, halved
1/2 cup dry red wine
1/2 cup chicken broth or
   bouillon

1 plum tomato, peeled,
   seeded, finely
   chopped

2 tablespoons
   cornstarch
2 tablespoons cold
   water

Place chicken in slow-cooker. Add cooked bacon,
shallots, garlic, parsley, bay leaf, thyme, salt, pepper,
onions, mushrooms, wine, broth or bouillon and
tomato. Cover and cook on LOW 8 to 9 hours.
Remove chicken and vegetables with slotted spoon.
Discard bay leaf. Turn pot on HIGH. Dissolve
cornstarch in water; stir into juices in pot. Cover;
cook on HIGH 20 to 30 minutes, stirring occasionally.
Pour over chicken mixture. Makes about 5 servings.

1 serving contains:

Cal	Prot	Carb	Fat	Chol	Sodium
367	47g	10g	13g	136mg	321mg

A welcome dish for any time of the year.

TORTILLA STACK

Thanks to convenience foods, this dish is easily put together and delicious tasting.

1½ lbs. lean ground
   beef
8 corn tortillas, each cut
   into 6 wedges
1 can Cheddar cheese
   soup, undiluted
1 pkg. taco seasoning
   mix (dry)
3 medium tomatoes,
   chopped

¼ cup dairy sour cream
2 cups shredded lettuce
¼ cup chopped green
   onion
1 red bell pepper,
   chopped
1 avocado, peeled,
   chopped

Crumble one-fourth of ground beef into bottom of slow-cooker. Top with one-fourth of tortilla wedges. In small bowl, combine soup and taco mix. Spread one-fourth of soup mixture over tortillas in pot. Sprinkle with one-fourth of tomatoes. Repeat layering until all ingredients are in pot. Cover and cook on LOW 4 to 5 hours.

Spoon onto individual plates. Top each serving with

sour cream, and shredded lettuce, green onions, bell pepper and avocado. Makes 6 or 7 servings.

1 serving contains:

Cal	Prot	Carb	Fat	Chol	Sodium
372	21g	25g	23g	67mg	387mg

MOROCCAN HENS

For a more authentic North African menu, substitute couscous for rice.

2 Cornish hens, thawed, halved
1 garlic clove, crushed
1 tablespoon honey
¼ teaspoon ground turmeric
1 teaspoon grated onion
½ teaspoon ground allspice
¼ teaspoon salt
¹⁄₁₆ teaspoon cayenne
1 large tomato, peeled, seeded, chopped

Cooked rice
1 tablespoon toasted sesame seeds

Rinse hens; pat dry. In small bowl, combine garlic, honey, turmeric, onion, allspice, salt and cayenne. Brush on chicken; cover and refrigerate at least 4 hours. Place in slow-cooker with juice from marinade; sprinkle tomatoes over top. Cover; cook on LOW 5½ to 6 hours. Arrange on serving plate over cooked rice. Sprinkle with toasted sesame seeds. Makes 4 servings.

1 serving contains:

Cal	Prot	Carb	Fat	Chol	Sodium
240	32g	7g	9g	94mg	217mg

ALSATIAN-STYLE CHOUCROUTE

Slow-cooker version of the meal-in-a-dish that's a tradition in the Alsace area of France.

27 to 30 oz. refrigerated
  or canned sauerkraut
1 medium cooking
  apple, peeled,
  seeded, chopped

1 medium onion,
  chopped
1 carrot, shredded
8 juniper berries
1 bay leaf

1 tablespoon chopped
   fresh parsley
3 pork chops, boned,
   halved
6 slices (about ¹/₂ lb.)
   Canadian bacon
¹/₂ lb. smoked sausage,
   cut into 6 or 8 pieces

¹/₄ lb. hot Italian
   sausage, sliced
¹/₂ cup dry white wine
1 cup chicken broth or
   bouillon

Cooked new potatoes

Drain sauerkraut in colander or strainer. Rinse; drain
again. In slow-cooker, arrange alternate layers of
drained sauerkraut, apple, onion and carrot. Tie
juniper berries, bay leaf and parsley in cheesecloth;
add to pot. Top with pork chops, Canadian bacon,
smoked sausage and Italian sausage. Pour wine and
chicken broth or bouillon over ingredients in pot.
Cover and cook on LOW 6 to 8 hours. Remove and
discard spice bag. With slotted spoon, place
sauerkraut and vegetables in center of large platter.
Arrange meats over and around vegetables. Serve with
cooked new potatoes. Makes 6 to 8 servings.

1 serving contains:

Cal	Prot	Carb	Fat	Chol	Sodium
277	19g	9g	17g	63mg	1320mg

ITALIAN-STYLE BEAN SOUP

*You may be surprised if the mushrooms turn dark,
but you'll like the flavor.*

1 cup small dried white
   beans, rinsed
6 cups chicken broth or
   bouillon
1 onion, chopped
1/2 cup chopped fennel
1 teaspoon chopped
   fresh thyme
1 bay leaf

6 mushrooms, coarsely
   chopped
1/4 teaspoon pepper
2 oz. (about 1/3 cup)
   prosciutto, chopped

1/4 cup dry white wine
Fennel leaves

In slow-cooker, combine beans, broth or bouillon,
onion, chopped fennel, thyme, bay leaf, mushrooms,
pepper and prosciutto. Cover and cook on LOW 7 to
8 hours or until beans are tender. Remove and discard
bay leaf. Stir in wine. Garnish each serving with a
sprig of fennel. Makes 6 or 7 servings.

1 serving contains:

Cal	Prot	Carb	Fat	Chol	Sodium
132	11g	16g	2g	5mg	117mg

CASSOULET,
THE CROCKERY WAY

Mild Italian sausage can be substituted if you prefer a less spicy dish.

1 lb. dried great
    Northern beans,
    rinsed
1 large onion,
    chopped
¼ teaspoon pepper
1 garlic clove, crushed
1 tablespoon chopped
    fresh parsley
2 whole cloves
1 bay leaf
1 sprig fresh thyme

¼ lb. salt pork, diced
1 lb. boneless lamb, cut
    into 1-inch cubes
½ lb. hot Italian
    sausage, crumbled
2 medium tomatoes,
    peeled, seeded,
    chopped
3 cups beef broth or
    bouillon
1 cup dry red wine

In slow-cooker, combine beans, onion, pepper, garlic and parsley. Wrap cloves, bay leaf and thyme in cheesecloth or metal tea container. Add to pot. Add salt pork, lamb, sausage and tomatoes. Pour beef broth or bouillon and wine over all. Cover; cook on LOW 9

to 10 hours. Remove and discard spice bag. Makes 6
to 7 servings.

1 serving contains:

Cal	Prot	Carb	Fat	Chol	Sodium
483	39g	31g	20g	92mg	473mg

*Several villages in Southwest France insist they
originated Cassoulet (ka su lay). Despite the
controversy we all enjoy this hearty dish.*

SLOW-COOKER & OTHER APPLIANCES

Your slow-cooker doesn't replace other appliances; it teams up with them to produce a wide variety of dishes. The microwave is handy for making sauces to go over dishes made in the slow-cooker. It can be used to reheat cooked meat and/or vegetables that you take out of the slow-cooker while you're thickening a sauce. Also the oven or toaster oven is handy for toasting nuts, pita rounds and sesame seeds.

Pasta and rice can simmer in a conventional pan on the stovetop before they're drained and added to other ingredients in the slow-cooker near the end of cooking.

Broil your favorite fish and transform it into a great dish by topping it with our Southwestern Sauce. Make the sauce ahead and quickly reheat in your microwave. Subtly flavored spaghetti squash and a crisp green salad complete your meal. Serve scrumptious Piña Colada Bread Pudding either warm or cold.

MENU

Broiled Fish
Southwestern Sauce, page 159
Spaghetti Squash
Green Salad
Blue Corn Muffins
Piña Colada Bread Pudding, page 67

TURKEY LASAGNE

A classic favorite with turkey replacing traditional ground beef.

³/₄ lb. ground turkey
1 small onion, chopped
¹/₂ cup chopped green
    or red bell pepper
1 garlic clove, crushed
2 (8-oz.) cans tomato
    sauce
1 (14¹/₂-oz.) can ready-
    cut peeled tomatoes
1 teaspoon chicken
    bouillon granules or 1
    bouillon cube

1 teaspoon chopped
    fresh oregano leaves
¹/₄ teaspoon salt
¹/₈ teaspoon pepper

¹/₂ lb. lasagne noodles
8 oz. ricotta cheese
8 oz. mozzarella cheese,
    sliced

In slow-cooker, combine turkey, onion, bell pepper, garlic, tomato sauce, tomatoes, bouillon, oregano, salt and pepper. Cover and cook on LOW 7 to 8 hours. Cook lasagne noodles according to package directions; drain. Preheat oven to 350F (175C). In 13″ × 9″ baking dish, arrange alternate layers of cooked lasagne noodles, hot turkey-tomato mixture, ricotta cheese and mozzarella cheese. Bake in preheated oven 30 minutes or until bubbly around edges. Makes 6 to 8 servings.

1 serving contains:

Cal	Prot	Carb	Fat	Chol	Sodium
324	24g	30g	13g	49mg	830mg

TROPIC TREASURE
BABY BACK RIBS

*A happy blend of traditional American seasonings
with flavors of the tropics.*

1 tablespoon grated
   fresh ginger root
1 garlic clove, crushed
2 tablespoons honey
1/2 teaspoon ground
   coriander
1/2 teaspoon ground
   turmeric
1/4 cup soy sauce
2 tablespoons white
   wine vinegar
1/4 cup ketchup
1/4 teaspoon salt

4 or 5 drops Tabasco®
   sauce
1 teaspoon instant
   chicken bouillon or 1
   chicken bouillon
   cube, crumbled
4 to 5 lbs. baby back
   pork ribs, cut into
   2- or 3-rib pieces

2 teaspoons sesame
   seeds

In small bowl, combine ginger root, garlic, honey, coriander, turmeric, soy sauce, vinegar, ketchup, salt, Tabasco® and bouillon. Brush both sides of ribs with sauce. Place in slow-cooker. Pour remaining sauce over all. Cover and cook on LOW 6 to 7 hours or until tender. With fork or slotted spoon, lift ribs from slow-cooker. Place single layer of drained ribs in shallow baking pan; brush with drippings in pot. Sprinkle with sesame seeds. Broil in oven until sesame seeds begin to brown. Makes 6 to 8 servings.

1 serving contains:

Cal	Prot	Carb	Fat	Chol	Sodium
375	26g	8g	26g	103mg	891mg

SOUTHWESTERN SAUCE

Use a 1-quart Crock-Ette® for this recipe or double the recipe and make it in a 3½- or 4-quart pot. You can keep sauce in refrigerator for a week, then reheat it at serving time.

4 medium tomatoes, peeled, seeded, chopped

3 medium tomatillos, husked, chopped

1 tablespoon vegetable oil

1 tablespoon minced green onions

1 jalapeño pepper, seeded, chopped

1 garlic clove, crushed

1 tablespoon red wine vinegar

1 tablespoon chopped fresh cilantro

¼ teaspoon salt

Broiled fish or chicken

Fresh cilantro leaves

In 1-quart slow-cooker, combine tomatoes, tomatillos, oil, onions, jalapeño pepper, garlic, vinegar, 1 tablespoon cilantro and salt. Cover and cook on LOW 3½ to 4 hours. Spoon over broiled fish or chicken. Garnish with cilantro leaves. Makes about 2¾ cups sauce.

1 tablespoon contains:

Cal	Prot	Carb	Fat	Chol	Sodium
7	0	1g	0	0	17mg

You'll find many uses for this sauce: topping broiled fish or poultry, adding zest to beans, roast beef or lamb sandwiches.

STUFFED ONIONS, SOUTHEAST-ASIA STYLE

Use the scooped-out pieces of onion to season other vegetable or meat dishes.

5 medium onions, peeled
½ lb. ground turkey
½ cup soft breadcrumbs
1 egg, beaten slightly
1 garlic clove, crushed
1 tablespoon soy sauce
1 tablespoon hoisin sauce
¼ teaspoon ground ginger

Plum Glaze:
½ cup plum jelly
1 tablespoon white wine vinegar
1 tablespoon ketchup
1 teaspoon Dijon-style mustard
Toasted sesame seeds

With sharp knife, cut about $1/2$-inch slice across top of each onion. Carefully cut out centers, leaving about $1/2$-inch sides and bottom. In medium bowl, combine turkey, breadcrumbs, egg, garlic, soy sauce, hoisin sauce and ginger. Spoon about $1/4$ cup stuffing into each onion shell. Place rack in slow-cooker, add $1/2$ cup water. Arrange filled onions on rack. If all onions do not fit on bottom of cooker, place 3 on bottom; lightly cover with heavy-duty foil. Arrange remaining onions on top. Cover and cook on LOW 7 to 8 hours or until onions are tender. Spoon Plum Glaze over onions. Makes 5 servings.

Plum Glaze: At serving time, combine jelly, vinegar, ketchup and mustard. Stir over low heat or in microwave until dissolved. Spoon over cooked onions. Sprinkle with sesame seeds.

1 serving contains:

Cal	Prot	Carb	Fat	Chol	Sodium
219	12g	29g	7g	69mg	380mg

REFRIED BEANS (FRIJOLES)

Guaranteed to be a hit as accompaniment to
enchiladas, tacos or other Mexican dishes.

1 lb. dried pinto beans,
  rinsed
1/4 teaspoon dried red-
  pepper flakes
1 garlic clove
1/4 lb. salt pork, cubed
6 cups water
1/2 teaspoon salt,
  optional

1 tablespoon vegetable
  oil

Shredded Cheddar
  cheese, optional

In slow-cooker, combine dried beans, red-pepper
flakes, garlic, salt pork and water. Cover and cook on
LOW 10 to 11 hours. Add salt, if desired. Partially
mash beans with potato masher or in food processor.
Serve now or refrigerate. Just before serving, heat oil
in large skillet. Add beans; heat and stir until fairly
dry. Top with cheese or serve plain. Makes 7 1/2 cups.

1 cup contains:

Cal	Prot	Carb	Fat	Chol	Sodium
226	12g	31g	6g	6mg	123mg

STUFFED ACORN SQUASH

Use "hot" or "regular" sausage, depending on your tolerance for spicy foods.

2 acorn squash, halved, seeded
1 tablespoon vegetable oil
½ lb. bulk sausage
1 egg, beaten slightly
3 slices raisin bread, toasted, coarsely crumbled
¼ teaspoon ground nutmeg
½ teaspoon Dijon-style mustard

1 orange, peeled, cut into 4 crosswise slices

Orange-Nutmeg Sauce:
1 tablespoon cornstarch
1 cup orange juice
1 tablespoon honey
1 teaspoon lemon juice
Ground nutmeg

Brush cut edges and inside squash with oil. In small bowl, combine sausage, egg, toasted bread, nutmeg and mustard. Spoon into squash halves. Place cut-side up on rack in slow-cooker. Top each with slice of orange. Cover pot, cook on LOW 5 to 6 hours or until squash is tender. Spoon Orange-Nutmeg Sauce over all. Makes 4 servings.

Orange Nutmeg-Sauce: In small saucepan or microwave dish, dissolve cornstarch in orange juice. Cook over moderate heat or in microwave until thickened. Stir in honey and lemon juice. Spoon over cooked squash. Sprinkle with nutmeg.

1 serving contains:

Cal	Prot	Carb	Fat	Chol	Sodium
529	13g	60g	29g	92mg	481mg

CURRIED CARROT BISQUE

*Mouth-watering flavors plus an appetizing golden
color guarantee a hit.*

8 medium carrots,
    peeled, chopped
1 onion, chopped
1 cooking apple, peeled,
    chopped
1 teaspoon curry
    powder
1 garlic clove, crushed
$1/4$ teaspoon ground
    coriander

$1/8$ teaspoon allspice
$1/4$ teaspoon salt
3 cups chicken broth or
    bouillon

1 cup milk or light
    cream
Chopped fresh cilantro
    leaves

In slow-cooker, combine carrots, onion, apple, curry
powder, garlic, coriander, allspice, salt and broth or
bouillon. Cover and cook on LOW 9 to 10 hours or
until carrots are very tender. Purée, half at a time, in
blender or food processor fitted with metal blade.
Gradually stir in milk or cream. Reheat in microwave
or in saucepan on stove. Sprinkle cilantro on top.
Makes about 6 cups.

1 cup contains:

Cal	Prot	Carb	Fat	Chol	Sodium
98	5g	16g	2g	4mg	143mg

Although there is a herb that's called curry plant, *the
curry powder we're familiar with is a blend of many
spices. Turmeric supplies the deep-golden color.*

TURKEY TROT STEW

Baked Cheddar Topping is delicious on Barbecued Beans 'n Beef, page 198 or Beef 'n Turkey Sausage Chili, page 52.

1 lb. dried black-eye
   peas, rinsed
2 cups chicken broth or
   bouillon
4 cups water
1 teaspoon ground
   coriander
1/2 teaspoon ground
   cumin
1 teaspoon ground
   cardamom
1 onion, chopped
1/8 teaspoon dried red-
   pepper flakes,
   crushed

1/2 teaspoon salt
2 (about 11/2-lbs.) turkey
   thighs, skinned

Baked Cheddar Topping:
11/2 cups boiling water
1/4 teaspoon salt
2/3 cup yellow cornmeal
1 egg, beaten slightly
4 tablespoons dairy sour
   cream
3/4 cup shredded
   Cheddar cheese

In slow-cooker, combine dried peas, broth or bouillon and water. Stir in coriander, cumin, cardamom, onion, red-pepper flakes and salt. Place thighs on top of dried peas and seasonings. Cover and cook on LOW 9 to 10 hours or until peas are tender. Remove thighs; cut meat into small chunks or shreds. Discard bones. Place meat and stew in casserole. Prepare Baked Cheddar Topping.

Baked Cheddar Topping: In medium saucepan, combine water and salt; gradually stir in cornmeal. Cook, stirring constantly, about 5 minutes or until thick. Remove from heat. Preheat oven to 375F (190C). Mix egg, sour cream and cheese. Gradually stir in cooked cornmeal. Drop in 9 mounds on top of cooked mixture in casserole. Bake 25 to 35 minutes or until topping begins to brown. Makes 8 to 9 servings.

1 serving contains:

Cal	Prot	Carb	Fat	Chol	Sodium
296	24g	30g	9g	69mg	280mg

VEGETABLE SMOOTHIE

Use your slow-cooker to prepare this dish the day before you're entertaining; then heat it in the oven just before serving.

5 medium potatoes, peeled, quartered

1 medium celery root, peeled, cubed

1 medium leek, trimmed, cut into ½-inch crosswise slices

½ teaspoon salt

⅛ teaspoon pepper

¼ teaspoon seasoned salt

4 cups water

½ cup milk or half and half

1 egg, slightly beaten

1 tablespoon minced parsley

¼ cup melted margarine or butter

In slow-cooker, combine potatoes, celery root, leek, salt, pepper, seasoned salt and water. Cover and cook on LOW 6 to 7 hours or until tender. Drain; mash with electric mixer or food processor fitted with metal blade. Add milk or half and half, egg, parsley and 3 tablespoons melted margarine or butter. Spoon into 1½-quart baking dish. Drizzle top with remaining tablespoon of melted margarine or butter. Bake in preheated 350F (175C) oven 25 to 30 minutes or until slightly browned on top. Makes 6 servings.

1 serving contains:

Cal	Prot	Carb	Fat	Chol	Sodium
197	5g	30g	7g	37mg	456mg

ALMOND GINGER APPLES

The meringue topping makes an interesting presentation but may be omitted, if desired.

6 large apples
1/4 cup almond paste
2 tablespoons powdered
  sugar
1 tablespoon minced
  crystallized ginger
1/4 teaspoon grated
  lemon peel
1/4 cup chopped toasted
  almonds

1 egg white
1/8 teaspoon lemon juice
1 tablespoon granulated
  sugar
2 tablespoons slivered
  almonds

With vegetable peeler, remove apple cores. In small bowl, combine almond paste, powdered sugar, ginger, lemon peel and chopped almonds. Spoon into center of each apple. Place in slow-cooker. If all apples do not fit on bottom of cooker, place 3 on bottom; lightly cover with heavy-duty foil. Arrange remaining apples on top of foil. Cover and cook on LOW 4 to 5 hours or until apples are done.

Just before serving, in small mixing bowl, beat egg white and lemon juice until foamy. Gradually beat in granulated sugar until peaks are stiff but not dry. Swirl on top of cooked apples. Place apples in broiler pan; sprinkle with slivered almonds. Broil until brown on top. Serve immediately. Spoon juice from slow-cooker over top, if desired. Makes 6 servings.

1 serving contains:

Cal	Prot	Carb	Fat	Chol	Sodium
182	3g	30g	7g	0	11mg

COOK TODAY—
SERVE TOMORROW

There are times when foods take all day or night to cook. As a result, it is important to consider when to start the cooking process so you don't have to get out of bed in the middle of the night to turn the pot off.

The foods in this chapter are cooked, then chilled before serving. That's good reason to let them cook one day, then refrigerate overnight for serving the next day. These cold soups and main-dish salads are welcome additions to summertime menus.

This homey menu combines our favorite Barbecued Beef Sandwiches and Traditional Baked Beans and promises you a carefree weekend. Prepare Barbecued Beef the day before; reheat in your microwave. Start your beans the night before and let them cook while you sleep. Cap the meal with fresh corn and rhubarb pie, which remind us of summer's bounty.

MENU

Barbecued Beef Sandwiches, page 177
French Rolls
Corn on the Cob
Traditional Baked Beans, page 91
Rhubarb Pie

COLD GREEN VICHYSSOISE

Plan ahead for adequate time to refrigerate this dish several hours or overnight.

5 medium potatoes,
 peeled, cut into 8ths
2 leeks, washed, sliced
 crosswise
1/4 cup fresh basil leaves
1 (10-oz.) pkg. frozen
 chopped spinach,
 thawed, drained
1/4 cup watercress leaves
3 cups chicken broth or
 bouillon

1/2 teaspoon seasoned
 salt
2 cups milk
1/2 teaspoon salt
1/8 teaspoon pepper

1 cup light cream
Fresh basil springs for
 garnish

In slow-cooker, combine potatoes, leeks, basil, spinach, watercress, broth or bouillon, seasoned salt, milk, salt and pepper. Cover and cook on LOW 6 to 7 hours or until vegetables are very tender. Purée in blender or food processor fitted with metal blade. Add light cream; refrigerate until cold. Ladle into individual bowls. Garnish with basil sprigs. Makes 8 servings.

1 serving contains:

Cal	Prot	Carb	Fat	Chol	Sodium
206	8g	28g	8g	26mg	283mg

Spinach and watercress supply both color and flavor.

CUP-OF-GOLD REFRESHER

Cook this soup the night before, refrigerate it during the day, then serve it cold for dinner.

3 apples, peeled, cored, chopped
6 carrots, peeled, chopped
1 small onion, chopped
1 tablespoon margarine or butter
2 teaspoons curry powder
1/8 teaspoon ground allspice

1/4 teaspoon salt
1/8 teaspoon pepper
3 cups chicken broth or bouillon

1/2 cup dairy sour cream
2 tablespoons toasted slivered almonds

In slow-cooker, combine apples, carrots, onions, margarine or butter, curry powder, allspice, salt, pepper and broth or bouillon. Cover and cook on LOW 9 to 10 hours or until vegetables are very soft. Purée, half at a time, in blender or food processor fitted with metal blade. Refrigerate at least 3 hours or until chilled. Stir in sour cream. Sprinkle with toasted almonds. Makes about 6 cups.

1 cup contains:

Cal	Prot	Carb	Fat	Chol	Sodium
161	5g	20g	8g	9mg	148mg

Smooth, cool and flavorful describes this wonderful, warm-weather dish.

COLD SUMMER SQUASH SOUP

A refreshing cold soup to make when summer squash is at the peak of garden-fresh flavor.

3 medium crookneck squash, sliced

3 medium zucchini, sliced

2 tablespoons sliced
  green onions
1 garlic clove, crushed
$\frac{1}{2}$ teaspoon salt
$\frac{1}{8}$ teaspoon pepper
3 cups chicken broth or
  bouillon

$\frac{1}{4}$ cup loosely packed
  watercress leaves

$\frac{1}{2}$ cup plain lowfat
  yogurt, stirred
$\frac{1}{4}$ teaspoon dried dill
  weed

Watercress sprigs for
  garnish

In slow-cooker, combine crookneck squash, zucchini,
green onions, garlic, salt, pepper and broth or
bouillon. Cover and cook on LOW 7 to 8 hours or
until squash is very tender. In blender or food
processor fitted with metal blade, purée hot vegetable
mixture with watercress, yogurt and dill until smooth.
Chill several hours or overnight. Serve in individual
bowls; garnish with watercress sprigs. Makes 6
servings.

1 serving contains:

Cal	Prot	Carb	Fat	Chol	Sodium
50	4g	6g	1g	2mg	194mg

BARBECUED BEEF SANDWICHES

The meat may be cooked a day ahead and refrigerated overnight. Skim solidified fat from top of sauce and meat. Reheat beef, shred and spoon on rolls.

2½ to 3 lbs. lean
  boneless chuck roast
¾ cup tomato ketchup
1 tablespoon Dijon-style
  mustard
2 tablespoons brown
  sugar
1 garlic clove, crushed
1 tablespoon
  Worcestershire sauce

2 tablespoons red wine
  vinegar
¼ teaspoon liquid
  smoke flavoring
¼ teaspoon salt
⅛ teaspoon pepper

10 to 12 French rolls or
  sandwich buns

Place beef in slow-cooker. Combine remaining ingredients, except rolls. Pour over meat. Cover and cook on LOW 8 to 9 hours. Refrigerate or prepare sandwiches now. Shred beef by pulling it apart with 2 forks; add 1 cup sauce. Reheat mixture in microwave or on stovetop. Spoon on warm, open-face rolls or

buns. Top with additional warm sauce, if desired.
Makes 10 to 12 servings.

1 serving contains:

Cal	Prot	Carb	Fat	Chol	Sodium
420	29g	42g	14g	75mg	711mg

SMOKED TURKEY
AND BEAN SALAD

*Add a crunchy French roll and a glass of iced tea for
a successful summer luncheon.*

1 cup dried pinto beans,
    rinsed

1 cup dried garbanzo
    beans, rinsed

¼ lb. smoked turkey,
    diced

4 cups water

2 tablespoons chopped
    fresh parsley

1 garlic clove,
    crushed

1 cup cooked green
    beans, drained

1/2 cup olive oil
1/4 cup white wine
    vinegar
1 tablespoon Dijon-style
    mustard
2 teaspoons honey
2 tablespoons chopped
    fresh chives
1/2 teaspoon dried dill
    weed

1/4 teaspoon salt
1/8 teaspoon pepper

1 small cucumber,
    peeled, diced
1/4 cup loosely packed
    watercress leaves
Lettuce
Chopped pimiento

In slow-cooker, combine dried beans, turkey, water, parsley and garlic. Cover; cook on LOW 10 to 11 hours or until beans are tender but firm.

Drain and discard liquid; cool drained bean mixture. Add green beans. In medium bowl, combine oil, vinegar, mustard, honey, chives, dill, salt and pepper. Pour over bean mixture; chill. Stir in cucumber and watercress. Serve in lettuce-lined bowl. Sprinkle with chopped pimiento. Makes 6 or 7 servings.

1 serving contains:

Cal	Prot	Carb	Fat	Chol	Sodium
319	12g	30g	18g	7mg	277mg

ANTIPASTO BEAN SALAD

Serve with sliced salami and mortadella plus a loaf of Italian bread.

1 lb. dried pink beans, rinsed

6 cups chicken broth or bouillon

1 garlic clove, crushed

¼ cup chopped celery leaves

½ cup olive oil

¼ cup vegetable oil

⅓ cup white wine vinegar

¼ cup loosely packed chopped basil

4 anchovy filets, chopped

1 red onion, thinly sliced

2 medium tomatoes, chopped

¼ cup sliced ripe olives

½ teaspoon salt

⅛ teaspoon pepper

Lettuce leaves

¼ cup (1 oz.) Gorgonzola cheese, crumbled

The day before serving, combine dried beans, broth or bouillon, garlic and celery leaves in slow-cooker.

Cover and cook on LOW 9 to 10 hours or until beans
are tender. Drain; refrigerate beans several hours or
overnight. Discard liquid. In large bowl, toss chilled
beans with oils, vinegar, basil, anchovies, onions,
tomatoes, olives, salt and pepper. Spoon into lettuce-
lined bowls or plates. Sprinkle with Gorgonzola
cheese. Makes 7 to 8 servings.

1 serving contains:

Cal	Prot	Carb	Fat	Chol	Sodium
398	15g	33g	24g	6mg	311mg

PINTO PEPPER SALAD

This colorful salad never fails to win admiration.

1 lb. dried pinto beans,
   rinsed
6 cups water

1 yellow or green bell
   pepper, seeded,
   chopped

1 fresh mild green chile
  or jalapeño pepper,
  seeded, finely
  chopped
1 small red onion, diced
2 cups cherry tomatoes,
  halved

1 cup thinly sliced
  fennel
2 cups bottled Italian
  salad dressing

Lettuce
Hard-cooked eggs

In slow-cooker, combine dried beans and water. Cover
and cook on LOW 9 to 10 hours or until beans are
done. Remove beans with slotted spoon; discard liquid
and refrigerate beans until chilled. In large bowl,
combine drained beans, bell pepper, chile or jalapeño
pepper, onion, tomatoes and fennel. Add salad
dressing; toss. Serve on lettuce. Garnish with wedges
of hard-cooked eggs. Makes 7 or 8 servings.

1 serving contains:

Cal	Prot	Carb	Fat	Chol	Sodium
449	10g	39g	36g	0	482mg

BLACK BEAN VINAIGRETTE

When buying ham hocks, try to find meaty ones with a minimum of fat.

1 lb. dried black beans, rinsed

7 cups water

2 ham hocks or 1 cup chopped ham

1 garlic clove, crushed

2 fresh jalapeño peppers, seeded, chopped

3/4 cup olive or vegetable oil

1/3 cup red wine vinegar

1/2 cup chopped red or yellow bell pepper

2 tablespoons chopped fresh parsley

1/4 cup chopped green onion

1/2 teaspoon salt

2 tablespoons capers

Lettuce leaves

2 hard-cooked eggs, chopped

The day before serving, combine dried beans, water, ham, garlic and jalapeño peppers in slow-cooker. Cover and cook on LOW 8 to 9 hours or until beans are tender. Cool to room temperature or refrigerate overnight. Drain thoroughly; discard liquid. If using ham hocks, chop lean meat; discard bones, skin and fat. In small bowl, combine oil, vinegar, bell pepper, parsley, green onion, salt and capers. Pour over beans; toss. Spoon into lettuce-lined bowl. Sprinkle eggs on top. Makes 6 to 8 servings.

1 serving contains:

Cal	Prot	Carb	Fat	Chol	Sodium
397	16g	29g	25g	64mg	435mg

Black beans, also called turtle beans, *have been a staple in Mexico and countries to the south.*

ZIPPY VEGETABLE DIP

If you're short of time, substitute packaged tortilla chips for pita or tortillas.

2 medium eggplants,
  peeled, cubed
¼ cup sun-dried
  tomatoes in oil,
  drained, chopped
1 garlic clove, crushed
1 onion, chopped
1 tablespoon chopped
  fresh Italian parsley
½ teaspoon chopped
  fresh thyme
1 tablespoon vegetable
  oil

½ teaspoon salt
¼ teaspoon pepper
¼ teaspoon crushed,
  dried red-pepper
  flakes

½ cup plain yogurt
2 teaspoons toasted
  sesame seeds
¼ cup sliced ripe olives
Wedges of toasted pita
  rounds or corn
  tortillas

In slow-cooker, combine eggplants, tomatoes, garlic, onions, parsley, thyme, oil, salt, pepper and red-pepper flakes. Cover and cook on LOW 6 or 7 hours or until vegetables are soft. With slotted spoon, scoop eggplant mixture into blender or food processor fitted with metal blade. Process until smooth. Stir in yogurt. Spoon into shallow bowl; sprinkle with sesame seeds. Garnish with olives. Scoop on wedges of toasted pita bread or tortillas. Makes 3¼ cups dip.

1 tablespoon contains:

Cal	Prot	Carb	Fat	Chol	Sodium
14	0	2g	1g	0	28mg

FARMER'S PRIDE RELISH

If fresh corn is not available, use ²/₃ cup frozen kernels and enjoy this old-time relish any time of the year.

2 ears corn
1 large green or red bell pepper, seeded, coarsely chopped
1 onion, chopped
2 cups thinly sliced cabbage
¹/₂ teaspoon dried red-pepper flakes
²/₃ cup white wine vinegar

¹/₃ cup sugar
¹/₂ teaspoon curry powder
¹/₂ teaspoon ground coriander
¹/₄ teaspoon ground turmeric
1 teaspoon dry mustard
¹/₂ teaspoon salt

Cut corn off cob. Combine in slow-cooker with bell pepper, onion, cabbage, red-pepper flakes, vinegar, sugar, curry powder, coriander, turmeric, dry mustard and salt. Cover; cook on LOW 6 to 7 hours. Cool and serve as an accompaniment to chicken or pork. Makes about 3¹/₂ cups.

1 tablespoon contains:

Cal	Prot	Carb	Fat	Chol	Sodium
9	0	2g	0	0	20mg

WINTER CHUTNEY

An unusual accompaniment to roast duck, chicken or pork.

3 pears, peeled, seeded, cut into chunks
1 cup dried fruit bits
2 tablespoons sliced green onion
2 tablespoons lemon juice
1 cup sugar

1 teaspoon grated lemon peel
1/4 teaspoon crushed dried red-pepper flakes
1 1/2 teaspoon slivered crystallized ginger

Combine in slow-cooker pears, dried fruit, green onions, lemon juice, sugar, lemon peel, red-pepper flakes and ginger. Cover and cook on LOW 3 to 4 hours. Cool. Makes about 3 cups chutney.

1 tablespoon contains:

Cal	Prot	Carb	Fat	Chol	Sodium
28	0	7g	0	0	1mg

Chutney is a relish that originated in East India. It usually combines sweet and sour ingredients. Both fruits and vegetables are teamed with herbs, spices and other seasonings.

QUICK AND EASY

Are you so busy getting the family off to school and work that there's practically no time left to make any dinner preparation before you leave for work? Then this section of the book is designed for you. There's a minimum of time-consuming pre-preparation to worry you.

Thanks to a variety of convenience foods, much of the tedious work is done for you. A package of pork chops or chicken pieces turns into a culinary marvel with very little time and effort on your part.

These recipes take the normal amount of cooking time in a slow-cooker, but the preparation time is shorter than usual.

How many times have you wished for a tasty, yet quick and easy meal? The answer is orange-flavored Sunshine Drumsticks or you may choose Shortcut Spareribs. Quickly cook frozen mixed vegetables and toss a salad while muffins heat. Top the meal off with chocolate cake.

MENU

Sunshine Drumsticks, page 195
Tossed Green Salad
Mixed Vegetables
Whole-wheat Muffins
Chocolate Cake

SHORTCUT SPARERIBS

For a more crispy texture, place single layer of cooked and drained ribs in shallow baking pan; broil in oven until brown on edges.

3 to 4 lbs. pork
  spareribs
1 cup bottled barbecue
  sauce

1 ($\frac{1}{2}$-oz.) pkg. dry green
  onion dip mix

Cut spareribs into individual ribs; place in slow-cooker. Combine barbecue sauce and green onion dip mix. Spoon over ribs. Cover and cook on LOW 6 to 7 hours or until ribs are tender. With fork or slotted spoon, lift ribs to platter. Makes 4 to 6 servings.

1 serving contains:

Cal	Prot	Carb	Fat	Chol	Sodium
494	34g	7g	36g	137mg	953mg

CROCKERY COOKER FAJITAS

If you prefer poultry, substitute 1 to 1 1/2 lbs. chicken or turkey, skinned and boned for the beef.

1 to 1 1/2 lbs. boneless
    beef round steak, cut
    in strips
1 red bell pepper, cut in
    strips
1 large onion, cut into
    thin wedges
1 (1-oz.) pkg. dry fajita
    mix

1/4 cup water

6 or 7 (7- or 8-inch)
    flour tortillas
2 small tomatoes,
    chopped
1 avocado, peeled,
    thinly sliced
1/2 cup dairy sour cream

In slow-cooker, combine beef, bell pepper, onion, fajita mix and water. Cover and cook on LOW 5 to 6 hours or until meat is tender. Warm tortillas in microwave or conventional oven. With slotted spoon, lift meat mixture out of pot. Place about 3/4 cup mixture along center of each tortilla. Top with chopped tomato, avocado and sour cream. Fold both sides over filling. Makes 6 or 7 servings.

1 serving contains:

Cal	Prot	Carb	Fat	Chol	Sodium
292	19g	22g	15g	54mg	155mg

Don't expect these fajitas to be "sizzling" and crunchy brown like those in many restaurants, but they are tender and tasty.

EASY SWEET-SOUR
PORK CHOPS

*For a change of pace, substitute chicken breasts for
this quick-to-fix pork dish.*

1 (16-oz.) bag frozen
Oriental-style
vegetables, partially
thawed

6 (about 2¼ lbs.) pork
chops

1 (2-oz.) pkg. sweet-sour
sauce blend mix

½ cup water

1 cup Chinese pea pods

Place partially thawed vegetables in slow-cooker.
Arrange pork chops on top. Combine sauce mix and
water. Pour sauce over chops and vegetables in slow-
cooker. Cover and cook on LOW 7 to 8 hours. Turn
on HIGH; add pea pods. Cover and cook on HIGH
about 5 minutes. Makes 6 servings.

1 serving contains:

Cal	Prot	Carb	Fat	Chol	Sodium
205	21g	12g	8g	58mg	69mg

POTATO LEEK
CHICKEN THIGHS

Leek soup mix creates a sauce that emphasizes the basic flavor created by the sliced fresh leek.

5 medium potatoes, peeled, sliced	10 to 12 chicken thighs
1 medium leek, washed, thinly sliced	1 (1.8-oz.) pkg. leek soup mix
	1 cup cold water

Combine potatoes and leek. Place on bottom of slow-cooker. Arrange chicken over potatoes. In small bowl, combine leek soup mix and water. Whisk until well mixed. Pour over chicken. Cover; cook on LOW 5 to 6 hours or until chicken is tender. Makes 5 to 6 servings.

1 serving contains:

Cal	Prot	Carb	Fat	Chol	Sodium
442	34g	30g	20g	116mg	874mg

Serve with sliced tomatoes and hot biscuits.

SUNSHINE DRUMSTICKS

*For a stronger citrus flavor, add 1 (8 oz.) can
drained mandarin oranges to cooked sauce.*

12 chicken drumsticks,
    skinned
1 (6-oz. or 12-oz.) can
    frozen orange juice
    concentrate, thawed,
    not reconstituted
2 to 3 tablespoons
    honey

2 tablespoons quick-
    cooking tapioca
1 fresh mild green chile
    or jalapeño pepper,
    seeded, thinly sliced
¼ teaspoon salt
1 teaspoon dried onion
    flakes

Place chicken in slow-cooker. In small bowl, combine
orange juice concentrate, honey, tapioca, chile or
jalapeño pepper, salt and onions. Pour over chicken.
Cover and cook on LOW about 5 hours or until
tender. Spoon sauce over chicken. Makes 12
drumsticks.

1 drumstick contains:

Cal	Prot	Carb	Fat	Chol	Sodium
152	15g	12g	6g	48mg	92mg

Adjust the flavorings to your personal taste. Use the higher range of orange juice, honey and jalapeño for extra orange flavor, spice or sweetness.

HONEY-MUSTARD BARBECUED SHORT RIBS

Start with bottled barbecue sauce or your favorite sauce recipe, then add a few additional flavors to perk up short ribs.

3 to 3½ lbs. beef short ribs

1 tablespoon Dijon-style mustard

1 garlic clove, crushed

2 tablespoons honey

½ teaspoon salt

⅛ teaspoon pepper

1 cup bottled hickory smoke barbecue sauce

2 tablespoons	Cooked noodles
cornstarch	
2 tablespoons cold	
water	

Place short ribs in slow-cooker. In medium bowl, combine mustard, garlic, honey, salt, pepper and barbecue sauce. Pour over ribs. Cover and cook on LOW 6 to 7 hours or until tender. Refrigerate several hours or overnight. Skim any solidified fat from top. Remove ribs; heat in microwave or conventional oven. Dissolve cornstarch in cold water. Add to sauce from ribs. Cook and stir in microwave or on stovetop until hot and slightly thickened. Pour hot sauce over warm ribs. Serve on cooked noodles. Makes 6 to 8 servings.

1 serving contains:

Cal	Prot	Carb	Fat	Chol	Sodium
349	35g	9g	18g	102mg	507mg

BARBECUED BEANS 'N BEEF

*So easy to put together with canned beans and
bottled barbecue sauce.*

1½ lbs. round steak or
  beef stew meat, cut
  into ½-inch cubes
1 onion, chopped
½ cup finely chopped
  celery
1 yellow or green bell
  pepper, seeded,
  chopped
2 (15-oz.) cans pinto
  beans, drained

¼ teaspoon salt
1 cup bottled hickory
  smoke barbecue
  sauce

1 cup (4 oz.) grated
  Cheddar cheese,
  optional

In slow-cooker, combine all ingredients except cheese.
Cover; cook on LOW 7 to 8 hours or until meat is
tender. Top with grated cheese, if desired. Makes 6 to
8 servings.

1 serving contains:

Cal	Prot	Carb	Fat	Chol	Sodium
314	30g	32g	8g	61mg	363mg

PICANTE TOMATO PIZAZZ

Use mild or hot picante sauce depending on your tolerance for hot, spicy foods.

1 (8-oz.) jar picante
  sauce
¼ cup loosely packed
  cilantro leaves

2 quarts tomato juice
2 cups beef broth or
  bouillon

In blender or food processor fitted with metal blade, combine picante sauce and cilantro. Process until smooth. Pour into slow-cooker with tomato juice and broth or bouillon. Cover; cook on LOW 4 to 5 hours. Stir well; serve in mugs or coffee cups. Makes 9 to 10 servings.

1 serving contains:

Cal	Prot	Carb	Fat	Chol	Sodium
46	2g	9g	1g	0	728mg

A warm spicy drink, ideal for warming you on those cold days.

"NO CHOPPING" VEGETABLE SOUP

For variety and convenience, use thin strips of pork or beef that many supermarkets sell for stir-frying.

2 cups beef broth or bouillon
1 (14-oz.) can stewed tomatoes
1 (16-oz.) can kidney beans, drained
1 (10-oz.) pkg. frozen mixed vegetables
1 (10-oz.) pkg. frozen baby onions

1 lb. fresh boneless turkey strips
1 teaspoon chili powder
½ teaspoon salt
⅛ teaspoon pepper

1 cup crushed tortilla chips

In slow-cooker, combine all ingredients except tortilla chips. Cover; cook on LOW 8 or 9 hours or until vegetables are done. Serve in individual bowls; sprinkle with tortilla chips. Makes 7 to 8 servings.

1 serving contains:

Cal	Prot	Carb	Fat	Chol	Sodium
217	23g	22g	4g	39mg	497mg

HOT BAJA COFFEE

You can be assured that this specially flavored coffee stays hot in your slow-cooker.

8 cups hot water
3 tablespoons instant
  coffee granules
½ cup coffee liqueur
¼ cup Crème de Cacao
  liqueur

¾ cup whipped cream
2 tablespoons grated
  semi-sweet chocolate

In slow-cooker, combine hot water, coffee granules and liqueurs. Cover and heat on LOW 2 to 4 hours. Ladle into mugs or heat-proof glasses. Top with whipped cream and grated chocolate. Makes 10 to 12 servings.

1 serving contains:

Cal	Prot	Carb	Fat	Chol	Sodium
98	0	9g	3g	10mg	10mg

This delightful drink is good enough to be called dessert.

DOUBLE-CORN DUMPLINGS

A topping added to cooked food in a slow-cooker;
then cooked covered on HIGH in the slow-cooker.

³/₄ cup all-purpose flour
¹/₄ cup yellow cornmeal
2 teaspoons baking
   powder
¹/₈ teaspoon salt

¹/₂ cup fresh corn
   kernels
¹/₂ cup milk
2 tablespoons vegetable
   oil

In medium bowl, combine flour, cornmeal, baking
powder and salt. Stir in corn, milk and oil. Spoon on
cooked hot stew or chili in slow-cooker. Cover and
cook on HIGH 30 to 35 minutes.

1 serving contains:

Cal	Prot	Carb	Fat	Chol	Sodium
85	2g	12g	3g	1mg	100mg

ABOUT THE AUTHORS

Mable and Gar Hoffman, the best-selling cookbook team, have added *Crockery Favorites* to their long list of successful cookbooks. Their other cookbooks (published by Fisher Books) include *Ice Cream, Frozen Yogurt* and *Carefree Entertaining*.

Fifteen years ago the Hoffmans began developing recipes for slow-cookers, which resulted in *Crockery Cookery,* a best-selling cookbook which has remained available throughout the years and still enjoys widespread appeal. *Crockery Favorites* is a companion book with new recipes, menus, and ideas.

Five of Mable's cookbooks have won R.T. French Tastemaker Awards, the "Oscar" for cookbooks. Although Mable's name appears on most of their books, Gar has been an important contributor.

The Hoffmans own and manage Hoffman Food Consultants, Inc. They concentrate their efforts on food styling, recipe development, and writing. They travel worldwide gathering ideas and information about foods and cuisines.

INDEX